VEGAN COOKBOOK FOR TEENS

Vegan Cookbook for Teens

100 EASY AND NUTRITIOUS PLANT-BASED RECIPES

BARB MUSICK

PHOTOGRAPHY BY MARIJA VIDAL

ROCKRIDGE
PRESS

For general information on our other products and services or to obtain technical support, please contact our Customer Care Department within the United States at (866) 744-2665, or outside the United States at (510) 253-0500.

Rockridge Press publishes its books in a variety of electronic and print formats. Some content that appears in print may not be available in electronic books, and vice versa.

TRADEMARKS: Rockridge Press and the Rockridge Press logo are trademarks or registered trademarks of Callisto Media Inc. and/or its affiliates, in the United States and other countries, and may not be used without written permission. All other trademarks are the property of their respective owners. Rockridge Press is not associated with any product or vendor mentioned in this book.

Interior and Cover Designer: Emma Hall
Art Producer: Megan Baggott
Editor: Andrea Leptinsky
Production Editor: Mia Moran
Production Manager: Riley Hoffman

Photography © 2021 Marija Vidal. Food styling by Victoria Woollard
Author photo courtesy of Angela Prodanova

ISBN: Print 978-1-64876-028-0
eBook 978-1-64876-029-7

R0

"The greatness of a nation
can be judged by the way
its animals are treated."

—MAHATMA GANDHI

Contents

Introduction

Hello! My name is Barb, and I'll be your guide as you explore the world of vegan cooking. I've been vegan for over 10 years now, and I'm excited to share ideas, tips, and recipes with you. If you're reading this book, it's likely that you are either vegan or interested in adding more vegan foods to your plate. I went (and will always be) vegan because I love animals. Dogs, cats, cows, and elephants—I have a big soft spot in my heart for every one of them. There are other reasons people choose to go vegan or to eat more plant-based meals, too. Eating vegan reduces your carbon footprint and helps save the planet, and it can also make you healthier. Whether you want to be kinder to animals, the planet, or your own body, there's no wrong reason to go vegan!

I didn't learn to cook until I was in my 20s, but I firmly believe that cooking is an important life skill for any teen to have. It's especially important for vegan (or vegan-curious) teens, because it gives you the ability to create delicious and nutritious plant-based meals for yourself. We've all had to make a meal out of vegetable sides while everyone else at the table eats meat. That's fine, but it's not *fun*. Fun is being able to create tasty vegan food to nourish yourself, your friends, and your family. This book will show you that vegan cooking doesn't have to mean eating boring sprouts and salads. It can be fun, flavorful, and easy to master!

CHAPTER 1

It's Your Kitchen

When I first became interested in cooking, I wasn't sure where to start. Everything in the kitchen seemed a bit overwhelming. Did I need different-sized pots? How many knives should I have? Why are there so many kinds of spices? I had a lot of questions, but I was lucky I had an uncle and friends who were really great cooks, and they usually had the answers. Once I got comfortable with the basics, I had the confidence I needed to try more challenging recipes and techniques. One day I realized I knew what I was doing in the kitchen!

If I can do it, anyone can—including you! Even if you're new to cooking, this book will show you step-by-step how to make delicious vegan food. We'll go over common cooking terms, essential tools, and kitchen safety. We'll even touch on how vegans (even growing teens!) can get all the nutrients they need while still eating their favorite foods. Stick with it, and before long you'll be the confident cook who others come to with their questions.

First Steps

If you are new to cooking, the kitchen can seem like an intimidating place. So many appliances and utensils! I promise it's easier than it seems, and it only takes a little know-how to get started. Follow these steps to get yourself ready to start cooking.

Flip through the book and choose a recipe that sounds delicious. Start in the fridge and pantry and see what ingredients you already have on hand, then make a shopping list for the rest. Try to tag along on your family's next grocery trip and choose your own ingredients. It's a great way to bring the cooking process full circle.

Wear the proper attire. Wear something comfortable, cover up with an apron, and tie that long hair back.

Set out all your vessels and utensils before starting. This keeps you organized, and it's also a great reminder to read the entire recipe through before starting.

Measure out and prep all your ingredients up front, according to the ingredient list. If the ingredient list calls for "1 carrot, grated," that means you should grate the carrot *before* you start cooking. Other recipes instruct you to prep ingredients during inactive time, like when you are waiting for the oven to heat up.

COOKING BASICS

Cooking has its own terminology, and learning it will make reading recipes easier. Here are some common terms and definitions to get you started.

Bake: To cook using dry heat, like in an oven.

Beat: To stir the ingredients together vigorously.

Boil: To cook ingredients in boiling water.

Broil: To place the food directly underneath the oven's heating elements to brown it.

Chop: To cut into smaller pieces, usually between $1/2$- and $3/4$-inch in diameter.

Cube: To cut into a $1/2$-inch cube. It's more precise than chopping and usually larger than a dice.

Dice: To cut into small cubes. Small dice usually means $1/8$-inch cubes, and large dice usually means $1/4$-inch cubes. This cut is more precise than chopping.

Fold: To gently add an ingredient to a mixture by using a spoon or spatula to scoop the mixture up from the bottom of the bowl and over the new ingredient.

Mince: To cut into the smallest pieces possible—the tinier the better!

Puree: To mash or blend an ingredient until completely smooth.

Sauté: To cook in a small amount of oil over direct heat.

Simmer: To cook in a hot liquid that is bubbling but not quite boiling.

Slice: To cut large ingredients into flat pieces of a similar thickness.

Steam: To cook food using the steam coming from boiling water, rather than in the water itself.

Whip: To use a whisk to incorporate air into whatever you're mixing.

Whisk: A technique and the name of the tool used to quickly combine ingredients.

ESSENTIAL EQUIPMENT

Although there's no need for a shopping spree to stock up on kitchen equipment, there are a few tools I find very useful when cooking. The following are tools called for in the recipes in this book—tools that I own and use on a regular basis.

Baking dishes and pans

Baking dishes are usually glass or ceramic and rectangular or oval, and they can be used for making everything from casseroles to baked pasta dishes. I call for **1-quart**, **1.5-quart**, and **2.5-quart baking dishes** in these recipes. **Baking pans** are metal, usually square or rectangular, and used more for baked goods like cakes and breads. They are also good for creating bars that you want to cut into perfectly even portions, like the No-Bake Cereal Bars (page 28) that call for a 9-by-9-inch baking pan. This book also calls for a **loaf pan**, such as in the Italian Meat Loaf (page 92), as well as **muffin tins**.

Baking sheet

Also called a cookie sheet, a **baking sheet** is a metal rectangle with a small lip around the edge. It's used for baking cookies and bar-type desserts and also for roasting vegetables and baking things like tofu. Recipes calling for a **small baking sheet** refer to one that is roughly 10 by 15 inches, but others use the most **standard-size baking sheet**, which is roughly 11 by 17 inches.

Blenders and mixers

These are used to mix and puree foods. A **stationary blender** sits on your counter. A "stick" or **immersion blender** is one that you dip right into your pot or mixing bowl—there's no need to pour ingredients back and forth! You also might need a **hand mixer**, a small appliance with two detachable beaters that allow you to whip or beat ingredients together quickly. Or you can always use a **whisk**!

Colander and strainers

A **colander** is the funny looking bowl with holes poked through it. It will help you drain the water from cooked pasta without burning yourself. I also recommend a **fine-mesh strainer** (sometimes called a **sieve**) for straining small things, such as seeds, from food.

Dutch oven

This is a really heavy pot (usually made of cast iron) with a lid that can be used both on the stovetop and in the oven. This is great for recipes like "Grilled Cheese" Tomato Soup (page 35) where you make the soup on the stovetop and then finish it under the broiler.

Food processor

One of my favorite tools! You can use it to blend, but you can also use it to chop, dice, and grate fruits and veggies.

Knives

Having at least one good chopping knife is important, and having a few different types is even better. The most important are a **chef's knife** for cutting and chopping, a **serrated bread knife** for slicing bread and tomatoes without tearing them, and a **paring knife** for peeling, slicing, and removing seeds from fruits and vegetables.

Lidded jars

These are great for recipes like Peanut Butter and Chocolate Overnight Oats (page 27), but also for when you want to make smoothies ahead of time or for on the go! You can buy mason jars with lids, or you can simply rinse and reuse pasta sauce jars (that's what I do!).

Measuring cups and spoons

Make sure you have a **liquid measuring cup** (this will likely be glass or plastic with a handle and spout and lines up the side), a **set of dry measuring cups** (likely metal or plastic), and a **set of measuring spoons**. You can't measure ingredients properly without these items!

Mixing bowls

Having bowls in a variety of sizes is important because many recipes, especially those for baked goods, require you to mix some ingredients separately from others. It's also good if at least a few of your mixing bowls have covers for when you need to rest or refrigerate ingredients.

Peelers and graters

There are different styles of peelers, and any of them will work to get the tough skin off vegetables like potatoes and squash. I also recommend a **box grater** for grating veggies and cheese and a type of grater called a **zester** for when you need very small pieces, like taking the zest from citrus. Microplane is a popular brand of zester.

Saucepans

These pans can be used for boiling, sautéing, and all types of cooking. They are identifiable by their high sides and one long handle. It is useful to have them in at least small and medium sizes with lids.

Skillet with a lid

Also called a frying pan, the **skillet** is a flat-bottomed pan with a handle that is mostly used for frying and browning, but can also be used for other kinds of cooking. I call for a **large skillet** (14 inches or larger) and a **medium skillet** (between 8 and 12 inches) in these recipes. A large one is great for cooking ingredients in a single layer. When in doubt, use a larger skillet, as it is easier to cook when your ingredients aren't crowded. I also recommend having at least one **nonstick skillet** for making things like pancakes. With all skillets, heavier ones are better as they conduct heat more evenly.

Spatulas

These come in all different shapes and sizes, but the two most important kinds are **rubber (or silicone) scraping spatulas** and **flat turning spatulas**. Flat spatulas are used for flipping things in a pan (like pancakes) and for moving food from a dish to a plate. Rubber spatulas are great for mixing wet and sticky ingredients together, as they are designed to scrape the sides of bowls or pots.

Stockpot with a lid

The **stockpot** is a very important tool to have, used for boiling water, making soups and sauces, and making recipes that are too large to fit into a saucepan. **Stockpots**, also called pots, have two looped handles, one on each side, to make them easier to lift when full of heavy liquid.

Tofu press

The **tofu press** is a tool that allows you to easily and neatly remove the excess liquid from tofu in minutes. This lets you control the texture of your tofu. (The drier it is, the chewier and "meatier" it'll be.) Then you can add flavor, either through a marinade or by allowing the tofu to soak up a sauce while cooking.

Tongs

You'll want a pair of **tongs** to pick food out of boiling water or off a hot tray. They can seem tricky to use at first, but you'll get the hang of them before you know it.

Wood cutting boards

When choosing a **cutting board**, I always recommend going with wood for multiple reasons. They're softer than bamboo, so they won't dull your knives as quickly. Plastic cutting boards are problematic, as tiny slivers of the plastic can end up in your food.

RECOMMENDED INGREDIENTS

Here are some of my favorite ingredients that are called for in this book. I recommend all plant-based cooks keep these on hand!

Kala namak

Also called "black salt," this gives your foods an eggy flavor, making it perfect for tofu scrambles and other tofu-based dishes.

Nondairy milk

There are plenty of nondairy milk options to choose from based on flavor or dietary restrictions—such as soy-free or nut-free—so use your favorite in these recipes. My favorites are oat milk and cashew milk. Do be careful to choose an "unsweetened" variety, as that is what these recipes call for.

Nonstick spray

These come in many varieties, so you can choose the one with the type of oil you like most (olive oil, avocado oil, etc.). Nonstick spray helps keep food from sticking to a pan, especially during baking.

Pure maple syrup

This is the all-natural maple syrup that comes from trees and has just one ingredient. Be sure to use the real stuff, not the "pancake syrup" brands that are full of corn syrup and artificial flavoring; these will cause your dishes to be much too sweet.

Salt

I have a variety of salts in my pantry, but most often I choose regular table or sea salt. If the recipe doesn't specify a particular kind of salt, use table salt.

Smoked paprika

Not to be confused with regular paprika, this version has a smoky flavor that tastes almost like bacon!

TIPS FOR SUCCESS

You should never feel bad if you make a mistake while cooking. It's part of the learning process, and we've all done it. Here are a few things to keep in mind to keep the mishaps to a minimum.

Measure ingredients properly. When measuring liquid ingredients, be sure to use a liquid measuring cup (the one with a handle and spout). I like to place the cup on the counter and pour the liquid into it until it reaches the desired measurement line. This keeps the cup steady and allows you to be precise. When measuring dry ingredients, use the small measuring cups that are identified by their amount (¼ cup, ½ cup, etc.) and always use a butter knife or something similar to level off the top.

Always set a timer. It's easy to get distracted in the kitchen, and a timer will keep your food from overcooking or burning.

Taste before adding additional seasonings. Adding more salt, chili powder, or other seasonings without tasting first can leave you with a dish that is just too salty or spicy to enjoy.

Read the entire recipe before starting. Although the recipes in this book are pretty easy, it's important to read the whole thing before starting for a couple of reasons. You want to make sure you have all the ingredients on hand, understand all of the steps, and have everything prepared correctly before starting.

SAFETY FIRST

Kitchen safety is not just important for teenage cooks—we all need to be careful! Most important, if you're confronted with an ingredient or situation you're not comfortable with, never be afraid to ask for help.

Cutting stuff

Learning to use knives correctly is one way to help guarantee your safety in the kitchen. Here are some tips to keep in mind.

× Choose the right knife for the task. Many knives are designed for a specific task or type of ingredient.

× Keep your knives sharp! Dull knives are actually more likely to slip and cause an injury. Ask the adult in your home about sharpening the knives in your kitchen.

× Never, ever cut toward yourself.

× When cutting, curl the tips of your fingers under to protect them.

× Use a cutting board for a more stable cutting surface. If it's slipping, try placing a damp dish towel underneath.

× Pay attention, take your time, and never be afraid to ask for help.

Handling hot stuff

You can't cook without heat, so keep these steps in mind to avoid being burned.

× Whether your stove is electric or gas, be mindful of the heat. Electric stoves with smooth flat surfaces can remain hot long after the burner has been turned off. Gas stoves have an open flame that can catch towels and shirtsleeves.

× Always keep oven mitts handy when baking or roasting. They are thicker and safer than using a towel and will help protect your wrists from the inside edges of the oven door. Wet oven mitts won't protect you from heat, so don't let your mitts get wet.

× Keep pan handles turned toward the back of the stove so they don't stick out over the edge. This can prevent bumping into them and burning yourself.

× Some pots and pans have handles that will get very hot. Use an oven mitt (or ask for help) when handling these.

Cleaning stuff

Keeping a clean workspace can make all the difference between a successful meal and a frustrating disaster. Keep these tips in mind.

× Prep the cook first! Wash your hands, make sure you have towels or an apron handy, and if you have long hair, tie it back.

× Clean up as you go! Washing your dishes and tools as soon you're done using them keeps your workspace clean and organized.

✕ Always wash your produce, even if it looks clean. Germs and dirt like to hide on veggies, and you don't want them in your food.

The Healthy Vegan

When you first decide to cut animal products out of your diet, you may wonder what you should be eating in their place. The good news is that it doesn't need to be confusing or complicated! Your body still needs the same mix of nutrients, from protein to vitamins, and there are lots of vegan options.

Science tells us that if we eat a varied and balanced diet of grains, legumes, veggies, and fruit we'll get all the nutrients our bodies need, but it's never a bad idea to be informed. Here are some vegan foods that can help you meet your nutrition goals.

Protein: It's an old joke among vegans that as soon as you announce you no longer eat meat, people will start asking where you get your protein. Tofu, lentils, and beans are examples of high-protein vegan foods, but did you know that nearly all fruits and vegetables contain at least some protein? It's true!

Iron: Our bodies need iron for growth and development, which is why it is an essential mineral. Lentils, chickpeas, beans, kale, and raisins are all foods with lots of iron. Many foods, such as breakfast cereals, are also fortified with it.

Calcium: Mostly known for keeping bones and teeth strong, calcium offers a variety of health benefits. Most plant-based dairy substitutes are fortified with calcium, but foods like kale and almonds are also good sources.

Vitamin B$_{12}$: This is one of the only vitamins that isn't produced by plants, meaning vegans must turn to fortified foods and supplements. Plant-based milks and margarines are often fortified with B$_{12}$, as is nutritional yeast. Talk to your doctor or your parents or guardians about supplements.

Omega-3 fatty acids: This fat supports our immune system, but our bodies aren't able to make it on their own, so we have to provide it through food or supplements. My favorite source of omega-3s is chia seeds, which also make a great egg substitute for baking when mixed with water.

WHY IT'S GREEN TO GO VEGAN

The food we choose to eat makes a huge difference on our effect on the environment. Raising animals for food requires an immense amount of water and land, and it also causes a lot of greenhouse gases. Our air and our water are being polluted, and that's scary, but there is something easy that you can do to help: eat more vegan meals! Eating vegan reduces your carbon footprint, even if you're not vegan full-time. Small steps like Meatless Monday and Tofu Tuesday make a difference, too. And if you're cooking delicious plant-based meals for your friends and family, perhaps they'll start to take these small steps with you!

About These Recipes

I tried to channel my inner teenager while developing these recipes, focusing on easy, delicious, nutritious dishes. Remember to always read the recipe carefully before you start cooking, and if there's a term you're unsure about, refer to the definitions earlier in this chapter or ask an adult.

Serving sizes vary throughout the book. Many chapters focus on meals for four, and there's an entire chapter dedicated to meals for one. Don't let the serving sizes keep you from trying a recipe though! You can double a recipe if you want to share Buffalo Chickpea Wraps (page 54) or Next-Level BLTs (page 59) with a friend. On the flip side, if you're craving Baking Sheet Fajitas (page 93) or Cashew Tofu (page 102), and you're the only one there to eat them, you can either divide the recipe to make less or simply store the leftovers in airtight containers to enjoy later.

As you're flipping through and deciding where to begin, keep an eye on the labels. Note that some of these recipes can be made nut- or soy-free if you buy cheeses that don't have those allergens in them. Here are the labels you'll see throughout the book:

5 ingredient: Uses only five or fewer main ingredients (not counting olive oil, salt, and pepper).

30-minute: Can be prepared, cooked, and served in 30 minutes or less.

Gluten-free: Does not contain gluten. Gluten can sometimes hide in vegan products, so be sure to always check the ingredient list! If you have a gluten allergy, always check the packaging for a "Gluten-Free" label, which indicates foods likes oats were processed in a completely gluten-free facility. (If not, they aren't truly gluten-free and should be avoided.)

Nut-free: Is free of nuts and coconut. Nut products can sometimes hide in vegan products, like spreads and dressings, so be sure to always check ingredient lists!

One-pot: Uses only one pot or pan.

Soy-free: Contains no soy products. Soy products can sometimes hide in vegan products, like spreads and dressings, so be sure to always check ingredient lists!

Most of the recipes also include special tips that will help you become a better cook, learn about ingredients, and make the dishes your own. There are the five kinds of tips you'll find in the following chapters:

Change It Up: For adding or changing ingredients to mix things up a little or try something new with the recipe.

Did You Know? Interesting background about a dish or a fun trivia fact about an aspect of cooking.

Ingredient Info: Info or advice on an ingredient's taste or how to cook it.

Kitchen Cure: A cooking tip to prep ahead, make something easier, save time, or fix a problem.

A FINAL WORD ON SUGAR

Many sugars are filtered through bone char, meaning they're not technically vegan. Look for an "organic" or "unfiltered" label for truly vegan sugar. Note that many vegans eat regular sugar, however, so the choice is up to you!

Tofu Scramble Totchos, page 19

Breakfast and Brunch

Baked Tofu Bacon

5 INGREDIENT
NUT-FREE

Serves 4

Prep time: 20 minutes, plus 30 minutes to marinate

Cook time: 30 minutes

1 (14-ounce) block firm or extra-firm tofu, pressed for at least 20 minutes

¼ cup real maple syrup

¼ cup soy sauce

2 teaspoons smoked paprika

½ teaspoon garlic powder

¼ teaspoon black pepper

Nonstick spray

There are plenty of good vegan bacon products in stores, but I recommend making your own! This version is smoky (thanks to the smoked paprika!) and chewy and oh-so-good on its own or in a dish like the Next-Level BLT (page 59).

1. **Prepare the tofu.** Halve the tofu lengthwise. Slice each half into 14 to 16 equal strips.

2. **Mix the marinade.** In a shallow bowl with a tight cover, combine the maple syrup, soy sauce, paprika, garlic powder, and pepper. Add the tofu and cover, flipping the container over a few times to coat the tofu. Refrigerate for at least 30 minutes, flipping a few times.

3. **Bake the tofu.** Preheat the oven to 375°F. Lightly spritz a baking sheet with nonstick spray. Lay the tofu on the sheet in a single layer (save the marinade!) and bake for 15 minutes. Spoon some of the leftover marinade over the tofu, then use tongs to carefully flip the pieces over. Spoon more marinade over the tofu, then bake for 10 to 15 minutes, until the tofu is crispy around the edges. The thinner you sliced the tofu, the faster it will get crispy.

Kitchen Cure: The more moisture you press from the tofu, the faster it will crisp up. If it's still soft after 35 minutes, try turning the broiler on low for about 1 minute, keeping an eye on it so it doesn't burn.

Apple Pie Pancakes

Serves 4
Prep time: 15 minutes
Cook time: 10 minutes

1¼ cups all-purpose flour

1 tablespoon brown sugar

2 teaspoons ground cinnamon

1 teaspoon baking powder

¼ teaspoon baking soda

¼ teaspoon nutmeg

⅛ teaspoon salt

1½ cups unsweetened nondairy milk

1 teaspoon vanilla extract

1 large apple

Vegan butter and real maple syrup, for serving

If you wish you could have dessert for breakfast like I do, this recipe will serve you well. All the flavors of apple pie, but in a pancake—and in 10 minutes!

1. **Mix the dry ingredients.** In a large bowl, whisk together the flour, brown sugar, cinnamon, baking powder, baking soda, nutmeg, and salt.

2. **Combine.** Add the milk and vanilla, stirring until just combined. Peel the apple and grate it with a box grater. Fold the shreds into the batter, which will have thickened during this time.

3. **Cook the pancakes.** Heat a large nonstick skillet over medium-high heat. It's hot when you sprinkle in a few drops of water and they "dance" in the pan. Use a ladle to transfer the batter into the pan. Make 2 to 4 pancakes at a time, making sure not to crowd the pan. Cook for about 2 minutes, until bubbles appear and pop. Flip the pancakes and cook for 1 to 2 minutes, until golden brown on the bottom. Serve hot with butter and syrup.

Ingredient Info: Crispy, slightly tart apples will work best here, including Fuji, Pink Lady, and Honeycrisp.

Sweet Potato Pancakes

Serves 4
Prep time: 15 minutes
Cook time: 20 minutes

2 medium/large sweet
  potatoes, scrubbed
1¼ cup all-purpose flour
1 teaspoon baking powder
¼ teaspoon baking soda
⅛ teaspoon salt
2 cups unsweetened
  nondairy milk
Vegan butter and real
  maple syrup, for serving

Pancakes are perfect for any meal, if you ask me—especially when they have sweet potatoes! In fact, I like to double the recipe just to keep some in the fridge for snacks.

1. **Microwave the potatoes.** Prick the sweet potatoes all over with a fork. Microwave for 8 to 10 minutes, turning over once, or until soft. Cool for a few minutes, then halve each potato and scoop out the insides. Measure 1 cup and set aside. Discard the rest with the skin.

2. **Mix the dry ingredients.** In a medium bowl, stir together the flour, baking powder, baking soda, and salt.

3. **Mix the wet ingredients.** In a small bowl, whisk together the 1 cup of sweet potato and the milk until combined. Pour this into the flour mixture, stirring until just combined. Let the batter sit for 2 to 3 minutes to thicken.

4. **Cook the pancakes.** Heat a large nonstick skillet over medium-high heat. It's hot when you sprinkle in a few drops of water and they "dance" in the pan. Use a ladle to transfer the batter into the pan. Make 2 to 4 pancakes at a time, making sure not to crowd the pan. Cook for about 2 minutes, until bubbles appear and pop. Flip the pancakes and cook for 1 to 2 minutes, until golden brown on the bottom. Serve hot with butter and syrup.

Oven-Roasted Breakfast Potatoes

GLUTEN-FREE
NUT-FREE
ONE-POT
SOY-FREE

Serves 4
Prep time: 10 minutes
Cook time: 30 minutes

5 large Yukon Gold
   potatoes
1 bell pepper (any color)
½ onion
2 tablespoons olive oil
1 tablespoon
   dried oregano
½ teaspoon garlic powder
1 teaspoon salt
¼ teaspoon black pepper
Hot sauce or real maple
   syrup, for serving
   (optional)

I call these potatoes "breaky taters." They are the perfect side dish for nearly any brunch or breakfast. If you don't have (or like!) a bell pepper or onion, the potatoes are still good on their own—especially with maple syrup or hot sauce!

1. **Chop the veggies.** Preheat the oven to 400°F. Cut the potatoes into bite-size pieces. Cut the bell pepper and onion into large dice.

2. **Season the veggies.** In a medium bowl, combine the potatoes, pepper, and onion. Add the oil, oregano, garlic powder, salt, and pepper, stirring until the veggies are coated.

3. **Bake.** Spread the veggies in a single layer on a baking sheet and bake for 15 minutes. Stir, then bake for another 10 to 15 minutes, until tender and crispy brown. Serve with hot sauce (if using).

Change It Up: Roasted potatoes make a great side dish for dinners, too! Skip the maple syrup and top with fresh herbs like rosemary and parsley.

Poblano-Sausage Hash

NUT-FREE
ONE-POT
SOY-FREE

When I serve brunch, this potato hash is always on the menu. The poblano adds a flavor that is smooth and smoky.

Serves 4
Prep time: 15 minutes
Cook time: 25 minutes

3 large Yukon Gold
   potatoes
1 poblano pepper
1 red bell pepper
½ sweet onion
4 vegan breakfast
   sausage patties
2 tablespoons olive oil
2 teaspoons
   dried oregano
½ teaspoon salt
¼ teaspoon black pepper
2 tablespoons water
¼ teaspoon minced garlic
Real maple syrup, for
   serving (optional)

1. **Prepare the veggies and patties.** Cut the potatoes into bite-size pieces. Remove the pith and seeds from the poblano pepper. Dice the poblano pepper, bell pepper, and onion. Quarter the sausage patties, then set everything aside.

2. **Fry the potatoes.** In a large skillet over medium-high heat, heat the oil. The oil is hot when it shimmers. Add the potatoes, oregano, salt, and pepper, stirring to coat. Arrange the potatoes in a single layer. Cover and cook, stirring occasionally, for 10 minutes, until the potatoes start to soften and brown.

3. **Add the veggies.** Using a spatula, move the potatoes to the outer edge of the pan, stacking them if necessary to make as much room as possible. Add the water, peppers, onion, sausage, and garlic. Cover and cook, stirring occasionally, for 5 to 6 minutes. This is called water sautéing. Add more water, 1 tablespoon at a time, if the pan gets dry.

4. **Serve.** Stir the potatoes into the veggies to combine. Cover and cook for 8 to 10 minutes or until the potatoes are soft and the sausage is cooked through. Taste and add more salt and pepper as needed. Serve with maple syrup (if using).

Ingredient Info: Most of the heat in a pepper comes from the pith and the seeds. Remove them to reduce the heat. Then, be sure to wash your hands.

Tofu Scramble Totchos

Serves 4

Prep time: 20 minutes
Cook time: 35 minutes

1 (16-ounce) block
   firm tofu

1 (16-ounce) bag frozen
   tater tots

1 tablespoon olive oil

½ teaspoon kala namak

¼ teaspoon black pepper

¾ cup favorite salsa, plus
   more for serving

½ cup canned black
   beans, rinsed

1½ cups vegan shred-
   ded cheddar or pepper
   Jack cheese

1 avocado, pitted, peeled,
   and sliced

Chopped fresh cilantro,
   diced red onion, vegan
   sour cream, and hot
   sauce, for serving
   (optional)

Nachos made with tater tots? You bet! This breakfast dish is always a crowd-pleaser.

1. **Prepare the tofu and tots.** Preheat the oven
   according to the tots' package instructions, usually 425°F. Meanwhile, press the tofu for at least
   20 minutes. Bake the tater tots according to package
   instructions, usually about 20 minutes. Set aside and
   set the oven to 350°F.

2. **Make the tofu scramble.** In a large skillet over
   medium-high heat, heat the oil until it shimmers.
   Crumble the tofu into the pan, then stir in the
   kala namak and pepper. Add the salsa and beans.
   Reduce the heat to medium-low and cook, stirring occasionally, for 3 to 4 minutes, until warmed
   through. Remove from heat (but leave the scramble
   in the pan).

3. **Layer the tots.** Spread the cooked tots on a baking
   sheet in an even layer. Pour the tofu scramble over
   the tots, then add the cheese. Bake for 5 to 10 minutes,
   until the cheese is melty. Let the tofu and tots cool for
   a few minutes.

4. **Serve.** Top with avocado slices and drizzle with
   salsa and other toppings (if using). Serve with
   lots of napkins!

Ingredient Info: Slicing an avocado is tricky.
Halve it lengthwise around the pit (ask for
help!). Gently hold on to each side and twist
until they separate. Use the tip of a spoon to
remove the seed, then scoop the fruit from
the peel and slice!

Jalapeño and Sweet Potato Tofu Scramble

Serves 4
Prep time: 15 minutes
Cook time: 30 minutes

Nonstick spray
1 large sweet potato
2 jalapeño peppers
Salt
Black pepper
1 (14-ounce) block
   firm tofu
1 teaspoon vegan butter
¼ cup unsweetened
   nondairy milk, plus more
   as needed
1 teaspoon ground cumin
½ teaspoon kala namak
½ teaspoon garlic powder
½ teaspoon ground
   turmeric

Kala namak is black salt with a superpower: it can make anything taste like eggs! But don't worry—regular salt works, too!

1. **Prep the tofu and veggies.** Preheat oven to 425°F. Lightly coat a baking sheet with nonstick spray and set aside. Meanwhile, cut the sweet potato into bite-size pieces and halve the jalapeños lengthwise. Remove the seeds and ribs, then cut the peppers into large dice.

2. **Bake the veggies.** Spread the sweet potato on the baking sheet in a single layer and spritz with nonstick spray. Sprinkle with salt and pepper. Bake for 15 minutes, then stir with a rubber spatula. Add the peppers and bake for 10 to 15 minutes, until the potatoes are tender with crispy edges.

3. **Make the scramble.** While the veggies bake, press the tofu for at least 10 minutes. Melt the butter in a large skillet over medium heat. Crumble the tofu into the pan. Using the rubber spatula, stir in the milk, cumin, kala namak, garlic powder, and turmeric. Cover and cook over low heat for 3 to 4 minutes, until heated through. If it gets too dry, add 1 to 2 more tablespoons of milk.

4. **Serve.** Remove the veggies from the oven. Use a regular spatula (not the rubber one) to add them to the scramble. Stir well and taste, then add salt and pepper, as needed.

Eggy Muffin Sandwiches

Serves 4
Prep time: 15 minutes
Cook time: 35 minutes

1 (12-ounce) block firm
silken tofu, drained but
not pressed

6 slices vegan cheddar
cheese, divided

¼ cup unsweetened
nondairy milk

1 tablespoon cornstarch

1 teaspoon Italian
seasoning

½ teaspoon kala namak,
plus more to taste

¼ teaspoon garlic powder

2 cups frozen broccoli,
thawed and
finely chopped

4 English muffins

Vegan butter, for
spreading

These sandwiches are healthier—and kinder to the environment—than their fast-food counterparts. Try them with a drizzle of hot sauce!

1. **Mix the "eggy" batter.** Preheat the oven to 350°F. Line a muffin tin with liners and set aside. Combine the tofu, two slices of cheese torn into quarters, milk, cornstarch, Italian seasoning, kala namak, and garlic powder in a food processor. Blend until smooth. Remove the blade and stir in the broccoli. Taste and season as needed.

2. **Bake.** Evenly spoon the mixture into the muffin cups and bake for 35 to 40 minutes, until firm, the tops are golden, and a fork poked into them comes out clean.

3. **Build the sandwiches.** Toast the muffins. Place the bottoms on an oven-safe plate, then spread with butter. Add three "eggs" and a slice of cheese to each one.

4. **Melt the cheese.** Broil the muffin halves on high for about 30 seconds, until the cheese is melty. Remove from the oven, top with the other muffin halves, and enjoy!

Kitchen Cure: The "eggs" can be made ahead of time and reheated when you're ready to assemble the sandwiches. Refrigerate in an airtight container and in the morning, you can just do steps 3 and 4 to create your sandwich!

Strawberry-Banana French Toast

Serves 4
Prep time: 10 minutes
Cook time: 15 minutes

8 to 10 strawberries,
  tops trimmed and
  thinly sliced

2 bananas (1 medium
  ripe and one very
  ripe), peeled

1½ cups unsweetened
  nondairy milk

1 teaspoon vanilla extract

½ teaspoon ground
  cinnamon

Vegan butter, for cooking
  and serving

8 slices day-old French
  bread, cut into ½-inch-
  thick slices

Real maple syrup,
  for serving

I thought I'd have to give up French toast when I first went vegan, but it wasn't true! It's easy to make with plant-based ingredients—and definitely just as delicious. If strawberries aren't in season, use your favorite fruit. Blueberries would be great!

1. **Prepare the fruit.** Place the strawberries in a small bowl. Thinly slice the less-ripe banana and add it to the bowl. Set aside.

2. **Mix the batter.** Place the riper banana in a medium bowl. Mash with the back of a fork, then whisk in the milk, vanilla, and cinnamon until smooth.

3. **Cook the French toast.** Heat a large pan over medium heat and melt just enough butter to coat the pan. Dip the pieces of bread into the milk mixture until both sides are completely coated, then place in the hot pan. Cook each side for 3 to 4 minutes, until lightly golden brown.

4. **Serve.** Plate the French toast and top with slices of fruit, vegan butter, and maple syrup.

> **Ingredient Info:** You may be wondering why it is important to use the riper banana in the batter. Bananas become sweeter as they ripen, so of course we don't want to eat green bananas. But they are also easier to mash and whisk into the batter, the riper (softer) they are.

Cheater Chilaquiles

Serves 4
Prep time: 20 minutes
Cook time: 15 minutes

For the tofu

1 tablespoon olive oil

1 (14-ounce) block firm
   tofu, pressed for
   20 minutes

1 cup vegan shredded
   cheddar cheese

1 tablespoon
   dried oregano

1 teaspoon ground cumin

½ teaspoon onion powder

½ teaspoon kala namak

½ teaspoon
   ground cayenne

For the chilaquiles

2 teaspoons olive oil

1 tablespoon minced garlic

2 (10-ounce) cans red
   enchilada sauce

1 (15-ounce) can black
   beans, drained
   and rinsed

½ teaspoon
   ground cayenne

Salt

Black pepper

5 cups tortilla chips

Traditional chilaquiles recipes call for fresh tortillas, but our version uses store-bought chips. It saves time, and the end result is just as delicious!

1. **Make the tofu scramble.** In a large skillet over medium-high heat, heat the oil until it shimmers. Crumble in the tofu, then stir in the cheese, oregano, cumin, onion powder, kala namak, and cayenne. Cook, stirring frequently, for 4 to 5 minutes, until the cheese melts. Taste and season as needed. Remove the tofu from the pan and set aside.

2. **Prepare the sauce.** Return the skillet to medium-high heat. Heat the oil until it shimmers. Add the garlic and cook for 1 minute, until fragrant and slightly soft. Add the enchilada sauce, beans, and cayenne.

3. **Cook the sauce.** Bring to a boil over high heat, then reduce the heat to low. Simmer, uncovered, for 5 minutes, stirring frequently. Turn off the heat, taste, and add salt and pepper as needed.

4. **Serve.** Fold the chips into the sauce (still in the skillet) and top with the tofu scramble.

Frozen Yogurt Breakfast Bites

Serves 4

Prep time: 15 minutes, plus 2 hours to freeze

Cook time: 1 minute

1 tablespoon plus
   2 teaspoons creamy
   peanut butter

1 tablespoon plus
   2 teaspoons real
   maple syrup

¾ cup favorite granola

Nonstick spray

1 cup vegan vanilla yogurt

½ cup blueberries

This fun take on breakfast is perfect for sharing with friends! If wrapped tightly, they'll last for up to two weeks in the freezer—just don't forget to let them thaw for 20 to 30 minutes in the fridge before serving.

1. **Prepare the granola.** In a microwave-safe medium bowl, microwave the peanut butter for 15 to 20 seconds, until very soft. Add the maple syrup and granola and mix until combined.

2. **Build the bites.** Line a muffin tin with 8 liners, then scoop the granola mixture evenly into the liners. Use the back of the spoon to firmly press down the mixture. If it's sticking to the spoon, wipe it clean and spritz it with nonstick spray. Add a layer of yogurt to each cup, then a sprinkling of the blueberries.

3. **Freeze.** Cover the muffin tin tightly with aluminum foil and freeze for at least 2 hours, being careful to keep the muffin tin flat. Thaw before enjoying!

Change It Up: Try these substitutions: use almond butter instead of peanut butter, fruit-flavored yogurt instead of vanilla, or diced strawberries instead of blueberries.

Summer Berry Fruit Salad

Serves 4
Prep time: 20 minutes

½ teaspoon lemon juice

½ teaspoon vanilla extract

2 teaspoons real
maple syrup

1 tablespoon orange juice

1 banana

1 Honeycrisp or Pink
Lady apple

6 to 8 strawberries

1 cup blueberries

This fruit salad is a vitamin-rich dish packed with sweet, mouthwatering flavors. It's a great addition to any breakfast or brunch.

1. **Mix the dressing.** In a medium bowl, whisk together the lemon juice, vanilla, maple syrup, and orange juice. Set aside.

2. **Prepare the fruit.** Peel and slice the banana into ¼-inch-thick pieces. Peel the apple or leave the skin on. Cut it into bite-size pieces. Remove the leaves from the strawberries, then cut them into bite-size pieces.

3. **Mix the salad.** Transfer the cut fruit and blueberries to the bowl with the dressing. Stir together until the fruit is evenly coated with dressing. Serve immediately.

Change It Up: Oranges or mandarins (peeled and chopped), raspberries, and blackberries are also great in this salad!

Kitchen Cure: Whisk together the dressing ahead of time and refrigerate it, but don't cut the banana or apple until you're ready to serve, so they don't turn brown.

Peanut Butter and Chocolate Overnight Oats

This classic duo brings a fun flair to overnight oats. If you'd like to eat them warm, simply heat them in a microwave-safe dish for 1 minute.

Serves 4

Prep time: 10 minutes, plus overnight to refrigerate

2 cups rolled oats

1⅓ cup unsweetened nondairy milk

¼ cup cocoa powder

¼ cup creamy peanut butter

¼ cup real maple syrup

½ teaspoon vanilla extract

¼ teaspoon salt

1. **Prepare the oats.** In a medium bowl, stir together the oats, milk, cocoa powder, peanut butter, maple syrup, vanilla, and salt. You want the peanut butter to be mixed thoroughly with the other ingredients.

2. **Refrigerate the oats.** Divide the oat mixture evenly into four Mason jars, cover tightly, and refrigerate overnight. Uncover and serve in the morning!

Ingredient Info: Rolled oats and old-fashioned oats are the same thing, and either will work in this recipe.

No-Bake Cereal Bars

5 INGREDIENT
GLUTEN-FREE
SOY-FREE

Serves 4

Prep time: 10 minutes, plus 45 minutes to refrigerate

Cook time: 2 minutes

¾ cup almond or
   peanut butter

¾ cup real maple syrup

4 cups favorite dry cereal

These cereal bars are perfect for switching up your breakfast routine. If you're using an all-natural nut butter, add ½ teaspoon of salt to the saucepan in step 1.

1. **Melt the nut butter.** Line a 9-by-9-inch baking pan with parchment paper and set aside. Heat a medium saucepan over medium-low heat, then add the almond butter and maple syrup. Stir with a rubber spatula for about 2 minutes, until the mixture is liquid.

2. **Add the cereal.** Remove the pan from the heat and stir in the dry cereal until combined.

3. **Shape and refrigerate.** Still using the rubber spatula, scrape the entire mixture into the prepared pan. Use the spatula to press the mixture down so that it is all one firm piece. Refrigerate for 30 to 45 minutes, until firm. Slice into pieces before serving. Tightly wrap the leftovers and store in the fridge for up to five days.

> **Change It Up:** There are so many ways to change the flavor of these bars, and it starts with the cereal you choose! You can use a fruit-flavored cereal to make it sweeter. Just make sure it's a flavor that pairs well with the nut butter you use.

Maple-Cinnamon Banana Bread

Makes 1 loaf
Prep time: 15 minutes
Cook time: 1 hour

Nonstick spray

1¾ cups plus
  2 tablespoons
  all-purpose flour

2 teaspoons
  baking powder

2 teaspoons ground
  cinnamon

½ teaspoon baking soda

¼ teaspoon salt

3 ripe bananas, peeled

½ cup real maple syrup,
  plus more for topping

⅓ cup unsweetened
  applesauce

1 teaspoon vanilla extract

Vegan butter and real
  maple syrup, for serving
  (optional)

Perfect for breakfast or a snack, banana bread is a great way to use up bananas that are starting to turn brown. I serve mine with a pat of vegan butter and a light drizzle of maple syrup!

1. **Mix the dry ingredients.** Preheat the oven to 350°F. Lightly coat a bread loaf pan with nonstick spray and set aside. In a large bowl, stir together the flour, baking powder, cinnamon, baking soda, and salt.

2. **Mix the wet ingredients and combine.** In a small bowl, use a fork to mash the bananas until there are no visible chunks. Whisk in the maple syrup, applesauce, and vanilla until fully combined. Pour this into the flour mixture. Mix until everything is just combined. The batter will be thick, and there may be some small lumps.

3. **Bake.** Pour the mixture into the prepared loaf pan. Bake for 50 to 60 minutes, until the sides of the bread begin to pull away from the pan, and a toothpick inserted into the center comes out clean. Cool for about 10 minutes in the pan, then slice and serve with vegan butter and maple syrup, as desired.

Did You Know? Bananas are one of the easiest vegan substitutes for eggs! They work in all sorts of recipes, especially when the banana flavor pairs well with the other ingredients.

Chocolate-Cherry Baked Oatmeal

Serves 4
Prep time: 15 minutes
Cook time: 40 minutes

Nonstick spray
½ cup pitted cherries
1 small banana, peeled
1 cup unsweetened
   nondairy milk
¼ cup vegan chocolate
   chips
3 tablespoons real
   maple syrup
2 tablespoons unsweet-
   ened applesauce
1½ cups rolled oats
1 teaspoon vanilla extract
1 teaspoon baking powder
¼ teaspoon salt

This tart-and-sweet breakfast treat will surely convert any skeptic into an oatmeal fan!

1. **Preheat the oven.** Preheat the oven to 350°F. Lightly coat a 1-quart baking dish with nonstick spray and set aside. Halve the cherries (it doesn't need to be perfect!).

2. **Mix the ingredients.** Use a fork to mash the banana in the bottom of a medium bowl, then stir in the milk, cherries, chocolate chips, maple syrup, applesauce, oats, vanilla, baking powder, and salt.

3. **Bake.** Pour the batter into the prepared baking dish and bake for 35 to 40 minutes, until the center is just barely soft and almost set. Cool for 3 to 4 minutes, then serve.

Lemon Chia Seed Muffins

Makes 8 muffins
Prep time: 20 minutes
Cook time: 25 minutes

2 tablespoons chia seeds

6 tablespoons water

⅔ cup all-purpose flour

⅓ cup whole wheat flour

⅓ cup sugar

1½ teaspoons
  baking powder

¼ teaspoon baking soda

¼ teaspoon salt

1 to 2 large lemons

2 tablespoons unsweet-
  ened nondairy milk

2 tablespoons vege-
  table oil

3 tablespoons unsweet-
  ened applesauce

1 cup powdered sugar

Chia seeds, like poppy seeds, add pretty little specks to this recipe all the while acting as the egg that holds the batter together.

1. **Make the chia "eggs."** Combine the chia seeds and water in a medium bowl. Stir well and set aside for 5 minutes.

2. **Mix the dry ingredients.** Preheat the oven to 375°F. Line a muffin tin with liners and set aside. In a large bowl, stir together the all-purpose and whole wheat flours, sugar, baking powder, baking soda, and salt.

3. **Mix the wet ingredients.** Zest the lemon over the bowl with the "eggs." Juice the lemon, measure out ½ cup, and set the rest aside. Add the milk, oil, ½ cup lemon juice, and applesauce, stirring to combine.

4. **Combine and bake.** Pour the wet mixture into the dry mixture, stirring until just mixed. Spoon the batter into the muffin cups, filling each about three-fourths full. Bake for 22 to 25 minutes, until a toothpick poked into the center comes out clean. Cool the muffins for a few minutes in the pan, then move them to a cooling rack.

5. **Glaze.** While the muffins are cooling, add the powdered sugar to a small bowl and stir briskly with a whisk or fork. Add 1 tablespoon of the reserved lemon juice and stir until a thin glaze forms. When the muffins are completely cool, use a spoon to drizzle the glaze over the tops.

> **Did You Know?** Chia seeds are high in fiber, protein, antioxidants, and omega-3s.

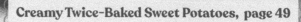
Creamy Twice-Baked Sweet Potatoes, page 49

CHAPTER 3

Soups, Snacks, and Sides

Baked Potato Soup

Serves 4 to 6

Prep time: 15 minutes

Cook time: 20 minutes

3 large russet potatoes

1 head cauliflower, cut into bite-size florets

2 tablespoons vegan butter

3½ cups unsweetened nondairy milk, plus more as needed

1 teaspoon garlic powder

½ teaspoon onion powder

1 teaspoon salt

¼ teaspoon black pepper

¼ teaspoon chili powder

1 cup frozen corn, thawed

3 scallions, thinly sliced, for topping (optional)

Shredded vegan cheddar cheese, diced vegan bacon (like Baked Tofu Bacon, page 14), and red pepper flakes, for topping (optional)

I love to eat this hearty soup on cold winter nights. Try my Baked Tofu Bacon or a store-bought version on top. Add anything you'd normally put on a baked potato!

1. **Cook and mash the potatoes.** Peel the potatoes and cut into ½-inch slices. Place them in a large pot along with the cauliflower florets, adding enough cold water to just cover the ingredients. Bring to a boil over high heat and cook for 12 to 15 minutes, until tender. Drain potatoes and cauliflower and return them to the pot.

2. **Combine.** Mash the potatoes and cauliflower until mostly smooth. Turn the pot's heat to medium. Stir in butter, milk, garlic powder, onion powder, salt, pepper, chili powder, and corn. Cover and let simmer 4 to 5 minutes until heated through.

3. **Serve.** Taste the soup for consistency. Add another ¼ to ½ cup milk to thin the soup as needed. Serve with a garnish of scallion or other toppings.

"Grilled Cheese" Tomato Soup

ONE-POT

Serves 4
Prep time: 15 minutes
Cook time: 25 minutes

1 tablespoon olive oil

½ teaspoon minced garlic

1 small sweet onion, diced

2 carrots, halved length-
    wise and cut into thin
    half-circles

½ cup vegetable broth

1 (28-ounce) can
    fire-roasted crushed
    tomatoes

½ teaspoon sugar

¼ teaspoon salt

⅛ teaspoon black pepper

2 cups unsweetened
    nondairy milk

2 cups vegan mozza-
    rella shreds

1 cup croutons

Lots of people enjoy pairing a grilled cheese sandwich with their tomato soup—but what if you could
get all of it together in one bowl? The gooey mozzarella and crunchy croutons will definitely make
you feel like you have!

1. **Cook the veggies.** In a Dutch oven over medium
   heat, heat the oil until it shimmers. Add the garlic
   and onion. Cook, stirring, for 2 to 3 minutes. Add the
   carrots and broth and cover. Cook, stirring occasionally, for 3 to 4 minutes.

2. **Simmer.** Increase the heat to high. Add the
   tomatoes, sugar, salt, and pepper and bring to a
   boil. Reduce heat to low, cover, and simmer for
   20 minutes, until the carrots are tender. Stir in the
   milk and simmer for 5 minutes. Remove from the
   heat. Taste and add more salt and pepper as needed.

3. **Blend.** Use an immersion blender to blend the soup
   until smooth.

4. **Add the cheese and broil.** Sprinkle the cheese
   evenly over the soup, then transfer the pot into the
   oven. While watching constantly, broil on high for
   30 to 60 seconds, until the cheese melts. Remove from
   the oven and serve in bowls topped with croutons.

Kitchen Cure: Dutch ovens are a great invest-
ment! Because they're so thick and heavy,
they retain heat and can be used for cooking
everything from soups to pastas to fried food.

Potato and Sausage Soup

NUT-FREE
ONE-POT

Serves 4
Prep time: 15 minutes
Cook time: 35 minutes

2 tablespoons olive
   oil, divided

2 precooked vegan Italian
   sausage links, cut into
   ¼-inch pieces (about
   ½ pound)

1 celery stalk, sliced

1 carrot, sliced

1 teaspoon minced garlic

3 medium Yukon Gold
   potatoes, cut into
   bite-size pieces

5 cups vegetable broth

3 tablespoons vegan
   Worcestershire sauce

2 teaspoons
   dried oregano

½ teaspoon red pepper
   flakes, or more
   as desired

½ teaspoon salt

¼ teaspoon black pepper

3 cups torn kale leaves

This hearty soup actually started out as a casse-role. Then one day I realized it would be better as a soup, and here we are. Never be afraid to follow your intuition and switch things up—you could end up with a new favorite dish!

1. **Brown the sausage.** In a medium saucepan over medium-high heat, heat 1 tablespoon of oil until it shimmers. Add the sausage. Cook for 2 to 3 minutes on each side, until lightly browned. Remove the sausage from the pan.

2. **Cook the veggies.** Return the pan to medium-high heat. Add the remaining 1 tablespoon of oil and heat until it shimmers. Add the celery, carrot, and garlic. Cook, stirring, for 3 to 4 minutes, until they smell really good.

3. **Make the soup.** Increase heat to high and add the potatoes, sausage, broth, Worcestershire sauce, oregano, red pepper flakes, salt, and pepper. Bring to a boil, then reduce the heat to low. Simmer, uncovered, for 20 minutes, stirring occasionally. Stir in the kale and simmer for another 3 minutes, until it has softened. Serve hot.

Southwestern-Style Chickpea Stew

Serves 4 to 6

Prep time: 15 minutes

Cook time: 30 minutes

1 tablespoon olive oil

1 bell pepper (any color), diced

½ onion, diced

1 teaspoon minced garlic

1 large sweet potato, peeled and cut into bite-size pieces

1 (15.5-ounce) can chickpeas, drained

1 (14.5-ounce) can diced fire-roasted tomatoes, with liquid

2 cups vegetable broth

2 teaspoons ground cumin

1½ teaspoons chili powder, or more as desired

1 teaspoon salt

½ teaspoon black pepper

1 small zucchini, cut into bite-size pieces

This stew is a great example of how delicious, healthy, and hearty veggies and beans can be. I always add more chili powder, but be careful—start with 1 teaspoon and taste before adding more.

1. **Cook the veggies.** In a medium saucepan over medium-high heat, heat the oil until it shimmers. Add the bell pepper, onion, and garlic. Cook, stirring, for 3 to 4 minutes, until the veggies soften.

2. **Make the stew.** Increase the heat to high. Add the sweet potato, chickpeas, tomatoes and their liquid, broth, cumin, chili powder, salt, and pepper. Reduce the heat to low and simmer, uncovered, for 20 minutes. Stir in the zucchini and simmer for 4 to 5 minutes, until tender. Taste and add more chili powder, salt, and pepper, as needed. Serve hot.

Change It Up: Want to feed more people, or make this stew more filling? Stir in 2 cups of cooked rice, quinoa, or couscous along with the zucchini, and add an extra ½ cup of broth or water to get the right consistency.

Quick Quinoa Chili

There are hundreds of ways to make chili—even vegan chili! This recipe is a quick and easy option when you have people to feed, and fast.

Serves 4
Prep time: 15 minutes
Cook time: 40 minutes

For the quinoa

1 cup quinoa, well rinsed
1½ cups water
⅛ teaspoon salt

For the chili

1 tablespoon olive oil
1 teaspoon minced garlic
1 (14.5-ounce) can diced
   fire-roasted tomatoes
   with chiles
1 (14.5-ounce) can
   tomato sauce
1 teaspoon ground cumin
½ teaspoon
   smoked paprika
½ teaspoon onion powder
½ teaspoon chili powder
   (optional)
2 (15-ounce) cans
   kidney beans, drained
   and rinsed
1 cup frozen corn
½ cup water, plus more
   as needed
Salt
Black pepper

1. **Cook the quinoa.** In a large saucepan over high heat, combine the quinoa, water, and salt. Bring to a boil, then reduce the heat to low. Simmer, covered, for 12 to 15 minutes, until all the water has been absorbed. Remove from the heat and let sit, still covered, for 10 minutes. Scoop the quinoa into a bowl and set aside.

2. **Cook the garlic.** Using the same saucepan, heat the oil over medium-high heat until it shimmers. Add the garlic and cook for 1 minute, until fragrant.

3. **Combine.** Stir in the quinoa, tomatoes with chiles, tomato sauce, cumin, paprika, onion powder, chili powder (if using), beans, corn, and water. Bring to a boil, then reduce the heat to low. Simmer for about 10 minutes, adding more water as necessary to get the consistency you want.

4. **Serve.** Taste and add salt and pepper as needed. Serve hot.

Crispy Coconut Tofu Bites

Serves 4

Prep time: 30 minutes, plus 20 minutes to marinate

Cook time: 30 minutes

1 (14-ounce) block extra-firm tofu, pressed for at least 30 minutes

¼ cup soy sauce

¼ cup brown sugar

1 teaspoon lime juice

½ teaspoon ground ginger

4 tablespoons cornstarch, divided

⅓ cup plus 2 tablespoons unsweetened nondairy milk

½ cup unsweetened coconut flakes

¼ cup panko bread crumbs

⅛ teaspoon salt

⅛ teaspoon black pepper

Nonstick spray

Sweet chili sauce, for serving

These tofu bites are baked, which is healthier and easier than frying.

1. **Marinate the tofu.** Cut the tofu into about 16 equal rectangles. Place them in a shallow bowl. In a small saucepan over medium-low heat, whisk together the soy sauce, brown sugar, lime juice, and ginger until the sugar melts. Cool for 2 to 3 minutes, then pour over the tofu. Marinate for 20 minutes, turning it over a few times, then pour out any remaining marinade.

2. **Prepare the breading station.** Preheat the oven to 400°F. Line a large rimmed baking sheet with parchment paper. Set out three shallow bowls. In one, place 3 tablespoons of cornstarch. In the next, whisk together the milk and remaining 1 tablespoon of cornstarch until the cornstarch has dissolved. In the third, mix the coconut flakes, bread crumbs, salt, and pepper. Arrange everything in a row: tofu, cornstarch, milk mixture, coconut mixture, and prepared baking sheet.

3. **Bread the tofu bites.** One at a time, roll a piece of tofu in the cornstarch. Using just one hand, dip it into the milk mixture until completely coated. Drop it into the coconut mixture. Switch hands and press the tofu into the bowl, turning it until all sides are breaded. Place the cube on the baking sheet, then repeat until all the pieces of tofu are breaded.

4. **Bake.** Lightly spritz the tops of the tofu with non-stick spray. Bake for 15 minutes. Use tongs to turn the pieces over. Lightly spritz the tops again with nonstick spray and bake for 10 to 12 minutes, until light golden brown. Remove from the oven and let sit for 5 minutes before serving with sweet chili sauce.

Cheeseburger Eggrolls

Serve 4
Prep time: 20 minutes
Cook time: 20 minutes

Nonstick spray

1¾ cups uncooked vegan ground beef (such as Impossible brand)

¾ cup vegan cheddar cheese shreds

½ cup diced dill pickles

2 tablespoons yellow mustard

1 tablespoon vegan Worcestershire sauce

½ teaspoon onion powder

8 vegan eggroll wrappers

Ketchup and/or vegan mayo, for dipping

I am an unapologetic lover of vegan "junk food," and these cheeseburger eggrolls are the treats I crave the most! I like to whip up a batch (or two!) for friends because they're such a delicious treat.

1. **Prepare the filling**. Preheat oven to 375°F. Lightly coat a baking sheet with nonstick spray and set aside. Heat a medium skillet over medium heat and cook the beef per package instructions, usually 8 to 10 minutes, until crumbly and fully cooked. Reduce the heat to low. Stir in the cheese, pickles, mustard, Worcestershire sauce, and onion powder. Remove from the heat.

2. **Build the eggrolls**. Fill a small bowl with warm water and place the wrappers on a clean, flat surface. Use a ¼-cup measure to scoop a heaping cup of filling into the center of each wrapper. Use your finger to rub all edges of each wrapper with water. Fold the two sides toward the center, then roll from the bottom up, like a burrito! Place the eggroll onto the prepared baking sheet, seam-side down, and repeat with the remaining ingredients.

3. **Bake the eggrolls**. Lightly spritz the top of the eggrolls with nonstick spray and bake for 18 to 20 minutes, flipping once halfway through, until the wrappers are crisp and light golden brown. Cool for 2 to 3 minutes before serving with ketchup or vegan mayo.

Ingredient Info: Most eggroll wrappers contain egg. Look for a vegan version. If you can't find any, use spring roll wrappers instead. They're thinner and more delicate, so you'll have to be a little more careful.

Cream Cheese Wontons

30-MINUTE
ONE-POT

Serves 4
Prep time: 15 minutes
Cook time: 15 minutes

Nonstick spray
½ cup vegan plain
   cream cheese
3 tablespoons thinly sliced
   scallions
1 teaspoon garlic powder
½ teaspoon ground ginger
12 wonton wrappers
Sweet-and-sour sauce,
   for dipping

I order Chinese food pretty often, but since none of the restaurants near me offer vegan wontons, I just make my own! They're so quick and easy I can make and bake them before dinner is delivered!

1. **Preheat the oven.** Preheat the oven to 400°F. Lightly coat a baking sheet with nonstick spray.

2. **Prepare the filling.** In a bowl, combine the cream cheese, scallions, garlic powder, and ginger. Mix well.

3. **Fill the wontons.** Fill a small bowl with warm water and place the wonton wrappers on a clean surface. Scoop exactly 2 teaspoons of the filling onto the center of each one. Use your finger to rub all edges of each wrapper with water. Fold the sides of the wrapper up so the corners create an "X," being careful to pinch all the edges together. Wet your fingers before pinching if the edges aren't sticking together.

4. **Bake the wontons.** Place the wontons on a baking sheet and lightly spritz the tops with nonstick spray. Bake for 10 to 11 minutes, until light golden brown. Serve with sweet-and-sour dipping sauce.

Kitchen Cure: You can make the filling up to two days in advance. Refrigerate in an airtight container until ready to use.

Easy Hummus

5 INGREDIENT
30-MINUTE
GLUTEN-FREE
NUT-FREE
ONE-POT
SOY-FREE

Hummus is usually made with tahini, which is a sesame paste with a strong flavor. Not everyone likes that flavor, so I skipped it and instead focused on items you are likely to have in your pantry! Serve with your favorite crackers, pretzels, or sliced veggies.

Serves 4
Prep time: 5 minutes

1 (15.5-ounce) can chickpeas

2 cloves garlic, peeled and roughly chopped

3 tablespoons lemon juice

1 tablespoon olive oil

½ teaspoon salt

1. **Drain the chickpeas.** Open the can of chickpeas and drain it over a bowl or measuring cup. Reserve the liquid.

2. **Mix the hummus.** Transfer the chickpeas to the food processor. Add 3 tablespoons of the reserved liquid. Add the garlic, lemon juice, oil, and salt and blend until the hummus is smooth and thick. Serve chilled or room temperature.

Ingredient Info: If you want really creamy hummus and have a few extra minutes, try removing the chickpea skins. Microwave the chickpeas for 30 to 40 seconds, then rinse them in cold water, rubbing them vigorously between your fingers.

Nacho Cheese Dip

30-MINUTE
GLUTEN-FREE
ONE-POT

Serves 4
Prep time: 10 minutes
Cook time: 20 minutes

2 medium Yukon Gold
   potatoes

2 carrots

⅔ cup unsweetened
   nondairy milk

½ cup nutritional yeast

2 tablespoons olive oil

2 teaspoons lemon juice

1½ teaspoons chili powder

1 teaspoon salt

1 teaspoon garlic powder

½ teaspoon onion powder

½ teaspoon ground cumin

1 or 2 teaspoons hot
   sauce (optional)

If you're new to vegan eating, you might be thinking, "Cheese made out of potatoes and carrots?" I get that, but stay with me. They provide the perfect base and texture for a cheese sauce, and once you've blended in all the seasonings, you'll be grabbing for the chips! Try it on the Ultimate Nachos (page 44).

1. **Cook the vegetables.** Peel the potatoes and carrots and cut them into 1-inch pieces. Place them in a medium saucepan and add enough water to cover them. Bring to a boil over high heat and boil for 8 to 10 minutes, until tender. Drain.

2. **Blend the cheese.** While the vegetables cook, combine the milk, nutritional yeast, oil, lemon juice, chili powder, salt, garlic powder, onion powder, and cumin in the blender. When the vegetables are cooked and drained, add them and blend on high until smooth. Use a rubber spatula to scrape down the sides so you don't miss anything. Taste and add hot sauce, if desired, blending for just another 2 to 3 seconds. Store in an airtight container in the fridge for up to three days.

Change It Up: Try using this in your next batch of mac 'n' cheese by mixing it with 2 cups of cooked pasta.

Ultimate Nachos

30-MINUTE
GLUTEN-FREE

Serves 4
Prep time: 15 minutes
Cook time: 5 minutes

1 Roma tomato

½ small red onion

1 jalapeño pepper

1 (15-ounce) can
   chili beans

½ teaspoon garlic powder

½ teaspoon chili powder

1 avocado

½ teaspoon salt

1 (10-ounce) bag
   tortilla chips

1½ cups vegan cheese
   sauce, warmed

This recipe is for nachos, one of my favorite options for lunch. Just keep an eye on your layering technique to get the most "bang" for your buck.

1. **Prep the veggies.** Dice the tomato and the onion. Remove the seeds and pith from the jalapeño, then cut it into large dice.

2. **Warm the chili beans.** Pour the beans into a medium saucepan over medium heat. Stir in the garlic powder and chili powder. Simmer for 3 to 4 minutes, until warmed through. Remove from the heat.

3. **Mash the avocado.** While the beans simmer, carefully halve, pit, and peel the avocado (see Tofu Scramble Totchos, page 19). Transfer the fruit to a small bowl and mash with a fork. Stir in the salt.

4. **Build the nachos.** Place about half of the chips on a large serving dish. Spoon about half of the bean mixture and half of the cheese sauce evenly over the chips. Add the rest of the chips on top, then layer on the rest of the beans followed by the rest of the cheese. Top with the tomato, onion, jalapeño, and avocado. Serve immediately.

Change It Up: Make these nachos even more ultimate by adding extra toppings, like vegan taco meat, vegan sour cream, and your favorite hot sauce.

"Cheesy" Bacon and Green Bean Casserole

Serves 4

Prep time: 15 minutes

Cook time: 40 minutes

Nonstick spray

1 (10-ounce) bag frozen French-cut green beans

1 tablespoon olive oil

½ teaspoon minced garlic

½ small yellow onion, diced

1 cup vegan shredded cheddar cheese

¼ cup unsweetened nondairy milk

¼ teaspoon salt

⅛ teaspoon black pepper

4 to 6 slices Baked Tofu Bacon (page 14) or cooked store-bought vegan bacon

¾ cup crispy French onions

It's the classic staple dish, complete with bacon and cheese—vegan, of course!

1. **Preheat the oven.** Preheat the oven to 350°F. Lightly coat a 1.5-quart baking dish with nonstick spray and set aside.

2. **Precook the green beans.** Add the beans to a medium saucepan and cover with cold water. Bring to a boil over high heat and cook for 3 to 4 minutes. Drain and set aside.

3. **Cook the veggies.** In a medium skillet over medium-high heat, heat the oil until it shimmers. Add the garlic and cook, stirring, for 1 to 2 minutes, then add the onion and cook, stirring, for 2 to 3 minutes, until softened.

4. **Make the cheese sauce.** Reduce the heat to medium-low. Add the cheese and milk. Taste, then add the salt and pepper as needed (some vegan cheeses are very salty). Add the bacon and green beans and stir until coated.

5. **Bake.** Spoon the green beans into the baking dish, cover with the French onions, and bake for 18 to 20 minutes, until golden brown and bubbly. Serve hot.

Sweet 'n' Spicy Corn Salad

Serves 4

Prep time: 20 minutes

For the salad

1 cup grape tomatoes

¼ red onion

1 large jalapeño pepper

1 red or orange
   bell pepper

1 small cucumber

3 cups sweet corn

For the dressing

1 lime

2 tablespoons real
   maple syrup

1 tablespoon olive oil

½ teaspoon chili powder

½ teaspoon salt

¼ teaspoon black pepper

The pepper's pop of heat combined with the sweetness of the corn and maple syrup makes this salad the perfect side dish at summer picnics.

1. **Prepare the veggies.** Quarter the tomatoes. Dice the onion, jalapeño, bell pepper, and cucumber. Transfer the cut veggies to a large bowl and stir in the corn.

2. **Make the dressing.** Use a zester to zest the lime over the veggies, then halve the lime and squeeze in the juice. Add the maple syrup, oil, chili powder, salt, and pepper. Stir until all the veggies are coated evenly. Serve cold or at room temperature.

Kitchen Cure: This salad can be made a day in advance and stored in an airtight container in the fridge. Be sure to stir well before serving.

(Just a Hint of) Maple Roasted Cauliflower

If you know someone who isn't sure they like cauliflower, try making them this. The hint of sweetness from the maple syrup combined with the nuttiness of the cauliflower go well together—and all vegetables are better when roasted!

Serves 4
Prep time: 15 minutes
Cook time: 25 minutes

Nonstick spray
3 tablespoons olive oil
1 tablespoon real
   maple syrup
¼ teaspoon salt
¼ teaspoon garlic powder
1 head cauliflower

1. **Mix the seasonings.** Preheat the oven to 425°F. Lightly coat a baking sheet with nonstick spray. In a small bowl, stir together the oil, maple syrup, salt, and garlic powder.

2. **Cut the cauliflower.** Cut the cauliflower into bite-size florets, then transfer them to the bowl. Stir until coated, then spoon them onto the prepared baking sheet in a single layer.

3. **Bake.** Bake for 20 to 25 minutes, stirring once halfway through, until the cauliflower is tender and a light golden brown on the tops and edges.

Did You Know? Cauliflower is a cruciferous veggie, in the same family as broccoli, cabbage, and Brussels sprouts. It's high in fiber, vitamins, and antioxidants.

Creamy Twice-Baked Sweet Potatoes

Serves 4

Prep time: 15 minutes

Cook time: 1 hour 10 minutes

2 medium sweet potatoes of similar shape

3 tablespoons vegan butter

1 tablespoon brown sugar

¼ teaspoon salt

¼ teaspoon ground cinnamon

Salt

Black pepper

Let's admit it: twice-baked potatoes are just fancy mashed potatoes. It's time to bring that shine to sweet potatoes!

1. **Bake the potatoes.** Preheat the oven to 375°F and line a baking sheet with parchment paper. Pierce the potatoes a few times with a fork and place them on the prepared baking sheet. Bake for 45 to 55 minutes, until tender. Remove them from the oven, but keep it on.

2. **Season the filling.** Wearing an oven mitt for heat protection, halve the potatoes and scoop the filling into a food processor or blender. (Be careful not to puncture the skin, as you're going to use that again in the next step.) Add the butter, brown sugar, salt, and cinnamon. Blend until completely smooth. Taste and add salt and pepper as needed.

3. **Refill the potatoes and bake.** Spoon the filling mixture back into the potato-skin shells. Bake for 10 to 15 minutes, until heated through.

Change It Up: Add steamed broccoli florets in step 3, before putting the potatoes back in the oven. You can also substitute 1 teaspoon cumin and ½ teaspoon chili powder for the brown sugar and cinnamon, and add black beans to give the potatoes a Tex-Mex flair.

Mashed Potatoes and Gravy

Serves 4

Prep time: 15 minutes

Cook time: 30 minutes

For the mashed potatoes

2 pounds Yukon Gold potatoes

4 to 6 tablespoons vegan butter

½ cup unsweetened nondairy milk, plus more as needed

½ teaspoon salt

¼ teaspoon garlic powder

For the gravy

2 cups vegetable broth

¼ cup all-purpose flour

½ teaspoon poultry seasoning

½ teaspoon salt

½ teaspoon dried parsley

½ teaspoon Dijon mustard

True story: When I was younger, I used to mix ketchup into my mashed potatoes to turn them pink! Ketchup is still my favorite condiment, but I definitely prefer mixing my mashies with gravy now—especially this gravy. It's thick and flavorful and really easy to make.

1. **Boil the potatoes.** Peel the potatoes and cut them into ½-inch slices. Place them in a large pot and add cold water to cover. Bring them to a boil over high heat, then cook for 12 to 15 minutes, until tender. Drain the potatoes, then return them to the pot.

2. **Mash the potatoes.** Add 4 tablespoons of butter, then the milk, salt, and garlic powder. As you mash the potatoes, make sure everything is fully combined. If the potatoes are too dry, add the remaining 2 tablespoons of butter or more milk, as needed. Taste and add more salt, as needed.

3. **Make the gravy.** In a medium pot, stir together the broth, flour, poultry seasoning, salt, parsley, and mustard. Stirring often with a whisk, bring the gravy to a boil over high heat, then reduce heat to medium-low. Cook, stirring, for 3 to 4 minutes, until the gravy thickens. Taste and add more seasonings, as needed. Serve over the mashed potatoes.

Agave-Garlic Roasted Vegetables

Serves 4

Prep time: 20 minutes

Cook time: 40 minutes

For the sauce

2 teaspoons cornstarch

1 tablespoon soy sauce

5 tablespoons vege-
table broth

2 tablespoons agave syrup

2 teaspoons garlic powder

Salt

Black pepper

For the vegetables

Nonstick spray

1 small red onion

1 bell pepper (any color)

2 cups Brussels sprouts

2 cups baby carrots

Honey and garlic are two flavors that go really well together, and you'll see them combined in a lot of recipes. Because most vegans don't eat honey, I've substituted agave syrup—a sweet syrup that comes from plants, not bees.

1. **Make the sauce.** Preheat the oven to 375°F. Lightly coat a 10-by-15-inch baking sheet with nonstick spray. In a small bowl, whisk together the cornstarch, soy sauce, broth, agave, and garlic powder. Taste and add salt and pepper, as needed. Set aside.

2. **Chop the vegetables.** Cut both ends off the onion, then halve straight down the middle. Cut each half in half again, then into quarters. Trim the stem end of the Brussels sprouts, then halve any large ones lengthwise. Chop the bell pepper into bite-size pieces.

3. **Roast the vegetables.** Spread the chopped veggies and baby carrots out on the prepared baking sheet, then pour the sauce over the top. Use tongs to stir so the veggies are evenly coated. Bake for 20 minutes, then stir with the tongs. Bake for 15 to 20 minutes, until the veggies are tender with golden brown edges. Use a spatula to scoop them from the baking sheet before serving. Taste and add salt and pepper, as needed.

Kitchen Cure: A small baking sheet keeps the sauce and vegetables together. If you're using a larger sheet, line it with aluminum foil and fold up the edges to mimic a 10-by-15-inch baking sheet.

Spicy Lentil Lettuce Wrap, page 71

CHAPTER 4
Meals for One

Buffalo Chickpea Wrap

30-MINUTE
NUT-FREE
ONE-POT
SOY-FREE

Makes 1 wrap
Prep time: 10 minutes
Cook time: 45 seconds

1 (15-ounce) can chick-
  peas, drained and rinsed

2 tablespoons vegan
  Buffalo sauce

1 ripe avocado

1 large tortilla

½ teaspoon salt

⅛ teaspoon black pepper

½ cup chopped lettuce

¼ cup shredded carrot

Buffalo sauce and avocado are two of the flavors I find most delicious, and this recipe combines them in one neat handheld meal!

1. **Prepare the chickpeas.** Measure out 1 cup of chickpeas (refrigerate the rest for another use). In a microwave-safe bowl, mix the chickpeas with the Buffalo sauce. Cover and microwave for 30 to 45 seconds, until warm. Use the back of a fork to smash some, but not all, of the chickpeas.

2. **Cut the avocado.** Carefully halve the avocado (see Tofu Scramble Totchos, page 19), but keep the pit in the half you're not using.

3. **Layer the wrap.** Place the tortilla on a flat surface. Use a butter knife to scoop out and smear the avocado evenly over the tortilla, except for the outer inch. Sprinkle with the salt and pepper, then pour in the chickpeas and top with the lettuce and carrot. Roll the tortilla up like a burrito and enjoy!

Kitchen Cure: When I have a leftover avocado half, I sprinkle it with sea salt and eat it with a spoon! Simply slide the tip of a spoon underneath the seed, then scoop it out and discard. To save the half for later, leave the seed in and cover with the empty avocado skin, being sure not to leave any of the green insides exposed. Wrap in plastic wrap and refrigerate for up to a day. Use it in the Epic Baked Potato (page 63)!

Jalapeño Popper Grilled "Cheese" Sandwich

**30-MINUTE
ONE-POT**

Makes 1 sandwich
Prep time: 5 minutes
Cook time: 5 minutes

1 small jalapeño pepper

2 tablespoons plain vegan
cream cheese, at room
temperature

⅛ teaspoon garlic powder

1 to 2 tablespoons
vegan butter

2 slices hearty bread

2 slices vegan
cheddar cheese

5 to 6 slices pickled
jalapeño peppers
(optional)

Jalapeño poppers are a popular appetizer for good reason! I love the spicy little peppers full of melty cheese. They can be time consuming to make, though. This "grilled cheese sandwich" version is easier and perfect for one. Don't forget to set the cream cheese out for a few minutes before beginning the recipe!

1. **Prepare the jalapeño.** Remove the stem, seeds, and pith from the jalapeño. Dice what remains, then transfer to a small bowl. Stir in the cream cheese and garlic powder.

2. **Build the sandwich.** Heat a medium skillet with a lid over medium heat. Spread the butter on one side of each slice of bread. Place one slice, butter-side down, in the pan. Top it with the cheddar cheese and pickled jalapeños (if using). Use a spoon to spread the cream cheese mixture on top, then place the remaining bread slice, butter-side up, on top. Cover with the lid.

3. **Cook.** Cook for 2 to 3 minutes, until the bottom slice of bread is golden and crispy. Use a flat spatula to carefully flip the sandwich, then cook for 2 minutes, until both sides are crispy and the cheese is melty. Serve hot.

Hearty Barbecue Sandwich and Slaw

NUT-FREE
ONE-POT

Makes 1 sandwich
Prep time: 20 minutes,
plus 30 minutes to chill
Cook time: 45 seconds

For the slaw

1 cup thinly sliced cabbage

1 small carrot

3 tablespoons
vegan mayo

½ teaspoon sugar

¼ teaspoon apple
cider vinegar

Salt

Black pepper

For the sandwich

Heaping ½ cup dried soy
curls (see page 69)

¼ cup barbecue sauce

1 tablespoon vegan mayo

2 slices bread

1 to 2 tablespoons diced
dill pickles

Creamy, tangy coleslaw and rich barbecue sauce are a great combination—and something great can be made even better by putting it on a sandwich!

1. **Prepare the slaw.** Cut the cabbage slices into 1-inch-long pieces. Grate the carrot using a box grater. In a medium bowl, stir together the mayo, sugar, and vinegar. Add the cabbage and carrots, mixing until evenly coated. Chill the slaw in the fridge for at least 30 minutes. Taste and add salt and pepper as needed.

2. **Soak the soy curls.** While the slaw chills, in a microwave-safe bowl, cover the soy curls with warm water. Soak for 10 minutes, then drain. Squeeze the remaining moisture from them with your hands. Tear any large pieces into halves or thirds. Stir in the barbecue sauce, then microwave for 30 to 45 seconds, until warm but not hot.

3. **Build the sandwich.** Spread the mayo on one side of each bread slice. Add the soy curls and as much slaw as you can. Top with the pickles, then add the other bread slice. Serve with the remaining coleslaw on the side.

> **Kitchen Cure:** Both the slaw and the barbecue soy curls can be prepared a day ahead and refrigerated in an airtight container. Wait until you're ready to eat before assembling the sandwich.

The Paris Baguette

5 INGREDIENT
30-MINUTE
ONE-POT

Makes 1 sandwich
Prep time: 10 minutes

1 tablespoon
   balsamic vinegar
1 tablespoon olive oil
⅛ teaspoon salt
Black pepper
1 (6-inch) baguette
1 (2-ounce) vegan
   mozzarella cheese ball
1 tomato
5 or 6 fresh basil leaves

I went to Paris for the first time in 2018, and everywhere I looked, street vendors and bakeries were selling baguette sandwiches. The locals ate them wrapped in paper while going about their day. They looked amazing! I never found a vegan version, so I created one.

1. **Make the dressing.** In a small bowl, mix the vinegar, oil, salt, and pepper. Set aside.

2. **Prep the ingredients.** Place the baguette on a cutting board and lay one palm on top to hold it still. Using a bread knife, halve the baguette lengthwise. Slice both the mozzarella and tomato into three or four (¼-inch) slices. (The bread knife works great on tomatoes!)

3. **Build the sandwich.** Lay the baguette halves cut-side up, then drizzle the dressing evenly over each half. Layer the basil, tomato, and mozzarella on one half, then top with the other half and enjoy!

Did You Know? I call this the Paris Baguette because that's where my inspiration came from, but you may notice that this meal looks a lot like caprese salad, a classic Italian dish made with fresh tomatoes, basil, and mozzarella.

No-Cheese Quesadilla

Makes 1 quesadilla
Prep time: 10 minutes
Cook time: 15 minutes

1 small sweet potato
  (about ½ cup mashed)
1 (15-ounce) can black
  beans, drained
  and rinsed
½ teaspoon ground cumin
¼ teaspoon salt
1 (10-inch) flour tortilla
Salsa, for serving

This quesadilla is the perfect meal when you don't have a lot of time to cook and you don't have any vegan cheese in the fridge! I usually have a small salad on the side.

1. **Prepare the filling.** Wash the sweet potato and poke small holes on two sides with a fork. Microwave for 4 to 5 minutes, turning over once, until you can easily stick a fork into its center. When it's cool enough to handle, scoop the filling out of the skin and place it in a small bowl. Measure out ⅓ cup of beans (refrigerate the rest for a later use) and add them, the cumin, and salt to the bowl and stir.

2. **Cook the quesadilla.** Heat a large skillet over medium heat. Place the tortilla flat inside the pan. Use a spoon to spread the potato mixture over half of the tortilla, then fold it in half. Cook for 3 to 4 minutes, until the bottom is golden brown. Use a flat spatula to carefully flip the quesadilla, then cook for 2 to 3 minutes, until golden brown. Cut into four slices and serve with salsa for dipping!

Kitchen Cure: This filling holds up well in the fridge, so try using a large sweet potato and a whole can of black beans, along with three times as much cumin and salt. Store the leftovers in an airtight container in the fridge for up to three days. You'll have enough for two more quesadillas!

Next-Level BLT

30-MINUTE
NUT-FREE
ONE-POT
SOY-FREE

Makes 1 sandwich
Prep time: 5 minutes

2 wide hearty bread slices

2 tablespoons
 vegan mayo

½ teaspoon
 yellow mustard

⅛ teaspoon black pepper

1 leaf green leaf lettuce

½ ripe tomato

3 slices vegan
 bacon, warmed

1 or 2 sandwich slice
 dill pickles

If you've never added dill pickles to your BLTs, you've been missing out! That bright, briny flavor goes so well with salty bacon. I like to whip up a batch of Baked Tofu Bacon (page 14) on Sundays and enjoy BLTs throughout the week when I don't have time to cook.

1. **Mix the secret sauce.** Lightly toast both pieces of bread. In a small bowl, use a fork to whisk together the mayo, mustard, and pepper. Cut the tomato into even slices.

2. **Build the sandwich.** Lay both pieces of bread on a plate. Schmear half of the secret sauce on each piece. On one slice, place the lettuce (breaking it into two pieces if you need to), tomato slices, bacon, and pickles. Flip the other piece over on top and enjoy!

Change It Up: If you don't like dill pickles but still want to take your BLT to the next level, slice up half an avocado and add that instead. Season with a little salt and pepper. Yum!

Chipotle Butternut Wrap

5 INGREDIENT
30-MINUTE
NUT-FREE
SOY-FREE

Makes 1 wrap
Prep time: 10 minutes
Cook time: 20 minutes

2 cups frozen butternut
squash cubes

1 tablespoon olive oil

1 teaspoon salt, divided

⅛ teaspoon black pepper

1 or 2 chipotle peppers
in adobo sauce, plus
½ teaspoon sauce
from can

1 pita

½ cup thinly sliced
cabbage, for topping

1 or 2 tablespoons vegan
sour cream, for topping

This wrap is so simple and quick to make. Butternut cubes are a great staple to keep in your freezer, and I definitely recommend keeping chipotle peppers in adobo sauce in your pantry. Most recipes won't use a whole can, so transfer what's left to an airtight zip-top bag and freeze it for next time.

1. **Roast the squash.** Place a baking sheet in the oven, then preheat it to 450°F. In a medium bowl, toss the squash with the oil, ½ teaspoon of salt, and the black pepper. When the oven is preheated, use oven mitts to carefully remove the hot pan and spread the squash out in a single layer. Bake for 10 minutes, then stir and bake for an additional 6 to 8 minutes, until the squash is tender with some golden brown edges.

2. **Season the squash.** Wipe out the bowl with a clean towel. Dice the chipotle peppers (be careful not to touch your face, and make sure to wash your hands afterward!). Transfer them to the bowl, along with the adobo sauce and the remaining ½ teaspoon of salt. Stir in the roasted squash and let sit for 2 to 3 minutes. Taste and add more adobo sauce if desired.

3. **Stuff the pita.** Halve the pita down the center. Gently scoop the squash mixture evenly into both halves, then top with the cabbage and sour cream. Enjoy!

Green Goddess Avocado Toast

5 INGREDIENT
30-MINUTE
NUT-FREE
ONE-POT
SOY-FREE

Serves 1

Prep time: 10 minutes

2 bread slices

6 cherry tomatoes

1 small ripe avocado

½ teaspoon sea salt
(optional)

1½ or 2 tablespoons vegan
green goddess dressing,
such as Gotham

Black pepper, for topping

This simple recipe yields maximum flavor! If you've never tried green goddess dressing, it's a creamy concoction of parsley, basil, and lemon flavors. It goes so well with sweet tomatoes and makes your avocado toast a little extra special.

1. **Prepare the ingredients.** Toast the bread. Quarter the tomatoes. Carefully halve, pit, and peel the avocado (see page 19). Transfer the fruit to a small bowl and mash with the back of a fork. Add the salt (if using) and mix to combine.

2. **Layer the toast.** Place the toast on a plate, then schmear the avocado evenly across both. Pile on the tomatoes, then drizzle with the dressing. Top with a sprinkle of pepper. Serve immediately.

Kitchen Cure: Some brands of green goddess dressing contain a lot of salt. To make sure your meal isn't too salty, taste the dressing before you add the salt to your avocado. You may not need it!

Leveled-Up Ramen

30-MINUTE
NUT-FREE
ONE-POT

Serves 1
Prep time: 5 minutes
Cook time: 4 minutes

2 cups water

1 cup frozen small mixed
   vegetables

1 (3-ounce) package
   instant ramen
   (any flavor)

4 teaspoons soy sauce

2 teaspoons hoisin sauce

½ teaspoon sriracha
   (or more)

¼ teaspoon ground ginger

1 tablespoon sliced scal-
   lions, green parts only,
   for topping (optional)

Packages of instant ramen have gotten a bad rap, but it's the seasoning packet that makes them high in sodium and chemical preservatives, not the noodles! That's why this recipe calls for tossing that seasoning packet in the trash and mixing up your own delicious flavor. Make sure you use small veggies, like corn or cut green beans, so they can cook quickly.

1. **Cook the veggies and noodles.** In a medium saucepan over high heat, bring the water to a boil. Add the vegetables and return to a boil. Cook for 1 minute. Add the dried noodles to the water (and toss the ramen seasoning packet in the trash). Cook for 3 minutes (or per package instructions), stirring two or three times, until tender.

2. **Drain and season.** Drain the noodle-and-vegetable mixture in a colander over a bowl. Return the noodles and vegetables to the pan, along with 1 cup of cooking liquid. Stir in the soy sauce, hoisin sauce, sriracha, and ginger until combined. Serve topped with sliced scallions (if using).

Did You Know? Ramen has been served in Japan since the 1600s, but many other Asian cultures have developed their own versions over the centuries.

Epic Baked Potato

5 INGREDIENT
30-MINUTE
GLUTEN-FREE
NUT-FREE
ONE-POT
SOY-FREE

I've been making a version of this meal since I was in high school. Sometimes I use vegan sour cream instead of avocado, and sometimes I melt some vegan cheddar cheese after adding the butter. It's always different, but it's always delicious!

Serves 1

Prep time: 10 minutes

Cook time: 55 minutes

1 medium russet potato

1 teaspoon olive oil

2 teaspoons vegan butter

Salt

Black pepper

½ avocado, mashed (see page 44)

1 or 2 tablespoons salsa

1. **Bake the potato.** Preheat the oven to 425°F and place a small piece of parchment paper (big enough for your potato) on a baking sheet. Use a fork to poke holes into the potato and place it on the parchment paper. Use your hands to rub the potato with oil. Bake for 45 to 55 minutes, until the inside is tender and the skin is crispy.

2. **Add toppings.** Use an oven mitt to pick up the potato and transfer it to a plate. Use a knife to slice open the top of the potato, then place the butter inside. (It helps to still be holding the potato with your oven-mitted hand.) Use a fork or spoon to stir the butter around inside. Sprinkle with salt and pepper. Spoon on the avocado and salsa and enjoy!

Change It Up: I'm not ashamed to share that sometimes I'm too hangry to wait for the potato to bake, so I microwave it. Still use the fork to poke holes, but skip the olive oil and cook it in the microwave for 8 to 10 minutes, turning over once halfway through, until tender.

Baked Buffalo Tofu Wingz

Serves 1

Prep time: 20 minutes, plus 1 hour to marinate

Cook time: 40 minutes

For the marinade

¼ cup vegetable broth

2 tablespoons soy sauce

1 tablespoon vegetable oil

For the wingz

Nonstick spray

1 (14.5-ounce) block extra-firm tofu, pressed overnight

½ cup cornstarch

1 teaspoon garlic powder

1 teaspoon poultry seasoning

¼ teaspoon salt

1¼ cup vegan Buffalo sauce

Celery sticks and vegan ranch, for serving (optional)

These tofu wingz will never trick anyone into thinking they're eating chicken, but that doesn't make them any less enjoyable! A big part of eating vegan is finding small adjustments that help animals and the environment, and this recipe is a great example of that.

1. **Mix the marinade.** In a shallow bowl with a lid, stir together the broth, soy sauce, and oil.

2. **Marinate the wingz.** Cut the tofu into thin finger-shaped rectangles. Place them in the marinade, cover, and refrigerate for 1 hour. If the lid is tight, try flipping the bowl over gently to ensure all the tofu gets marinated. Pour out any remaining marinade.

3. **Prepare the coating station.** Preheat the oven to 400°F. Lightly coat a baking sheet with nonstick spray. In another shallow bowl, mix the cornstarch, garlic powder, poultry seasoning, and salt. Place the marinated tofu, cornstarch mixture, and the prepared baking sheet in a row in front of you.

4. **Coat the wingz.** Using your left hand, pick up one tofu wing and drop it into the cornstarch. Switch hands and press all sides into the cornstarch until it is completely covered. Lay the wing on the baking sheet and repeat, keeping the finished wingz in a single layer.

CONTINUED

5. **Bake.** Lightly spritz the tops with nonstick spray and bake for 20 minutes. Spritz the tops again, then flip them over using tongs. Bake for another 15 to 20 minutes, until they are lightly golden brown.

6. **Dress and serve.** Move the wingz to a serving dish. Top with the Buffalo sauce, gently tossing to make sure they're all coated. Serve with celery and ranch (if using).

> Ingredient Info: Many national brands of Buffalo sauce are accidentally vegan. Just check the ingredients list for "milk" or "butter."

Flatbread Pizza

5 INGREDIENT
30-MINUTE
ONE-POT

Serves 1
Prep time: 5 minutes
Cook time: 10 minutes

1 (5- to 6-inch) naan or
flatbread

2 or 3 tablespoons
pizza sauce

¼ cup vegan mozzarella
cheese shreds, plus
more as needed

4 basil leaves

1 teaspoon nutritional
yeast (optional)

Salt

Black pepper

Making your own pizza means you never have to compromise on the toppings. I went with simple cheese and fresh basil here, but you can add anything you like. Even better, invite some friends over, lay out a variety of toppings, and let everyone make their own!

1. **Preheat the oven.** Preheat the oven to 400°F. Line a baking sheet with parchment paper.

2. **Bake the pizza.** Place the naan on the prepared baking sheet and spread the pizza sauce evenly over the surface. Top with the cheese and bake for 8 to 10 minutes, until the cheese is melted. Remove from the oven.

3. **Top the pizza.** While the pizza is baking, cut or tear the basil into smaller pieces. When the pizza is done, top with the basil and sprinkle with the nutritional yeast (if using). Finish with a sprinkle of salt and pepper and serve.

Ingredient Info: When stored with care, your basil can stay fresh and green for days. Wash and dry the leaves, then wrap them loosely in a dry paper towel. Store that in a sealed plastic bag in the fridge.

Avocado and Chipotle Chickpea Flatbread

Putting together a quick meal for yourself doesn't have to mean settling for a peanut butter sandwich. With the right ingredients on hand, you can whip up bright, flavorful meals like this flatbread in just minutes!

Serves 1

Prep time: 10 minutes

Cook time: 5 minutes

1 (15-ounce) can chickpeas, drained and rinsed

1 to 2 chipotle peppers in adobo, plus ½ teaspoon sauce

1 tablespoon olive oil

½ teaspoon lime juice

¼ teaspoon salt

⅛ teaspoon black pepper

½ avocado, pitted and peeled (see page 19)

1 (5- to 6-inch) naan or flatbread

1. **Prepare the ingredients.** Measure out 1 cup of chickpeas (refrigerate the rest for a later use). Dice the chipotle peppers (be careful not to touch your face, and be sure to wash your hands after).

2. **Season the chickpeas.** In a small pan over medium-low heat, heat the olive oil until it shimmers. Add the chickpeas, peppers and adobo sauce, lime juice, salt, and black pepper. Use the back of a fork to mash about half of the chickpeas (it doesn't need to be perfect). Cook for 4 to 5 minutes, until heated through. Taste and add more adobo sauce and salt as needed. If the mixture gets too dry, add water, 1 teaspoon at a time. You don't want it to be runny, but a little moisture is okay. Remove from heat but leave in the pan for now.

3. **Top the flatbread.** Cut the avocado into thin slices. Place the flatbread on a plate and spread the chickpea mixture evenly over it. Top with the avocado slices, then serve.

Fancy Chick'n Salad Sandwich

Makes 1 sandwich
Prep time: 15 minutes

½ cup dried soy curls

3 tablespoons
  vegan mayo

⅛ teaspoon apple
  cider vinegar

⅛ teaspoon salt

½ celery stalk

2 tablespoons sweetened
  dried cranberries

2 bread slices

Lettuce, for serving

When I was growing up, canned chicken salad was one of my favorite lunches. Soy curls make it easy to recreate—and this version is more fun because I've dressed it up with celery and dried cranberries.

1. **Soak the soy curls.** Place the soy curls in a microwave-safe bowl and cover with warm water. Let sit for 10 minutes, then drain. Squeeze the remaining moisture from them with your hands. Tear or cut any extra-large pieces into halves or thirds.

2. **Mix.** While the soy curls soak, in a small bowl mix the mayo, vinegar, and salt. Dice the celery and add it to the bowl, along with the cranberries and soy curls. Mix to combine.

3. **Build the sandwich.** Place one slice of bread on a plate and top it with lettuce. Spoon on the soy curl mixture and top with the other slice of bread.

Ingredient Info: Soy curls can be found at many health food stores as well as online. In fact, online shopping can be a great way to find lots of new plant-based products to try!

Roasted Veggie Tacos

Serves 1
Prep time: 10 minutes
Cook time: 30 minutes

1 Yukon Gold potato

1 small carrot

1 small jalapeño pepper

½ cup chopped cauliflower

2 teaspoons olive oil

¼ teaspoon salt

¼ teaspoon ground cumin

⅛ teaspoon chili powder

2 (6-inch) corn or flour tortillas

1 teaspoon lime juice

2 to 3 tablespoons salsa, for topping

Vegan shredded cheese, mashed avocado, and chopped fresh cilantro, for topping (optional)

Recipes like this—where you do most of the work and then put the dish in the oven—are great because they give you time to clean up the kitchen—or in this case, whip up a quick batch of guacamole to enjoy with the tacos!

1. **Chop the veggies.** Preheat the oven to 375°F. Line a baking sheet with parchment paper. Cut the potato and carrot into bite-size pieces. Remove the stem, seeds, and pith from the jalapeño, then cut into large dice. Transfer the potato, carrot, jalapeño, and cauliflower to a medium bowl. Add the oil, salt, cumin, and chili powder, mixing until everything is evenly coated.

2. **Bake.** Pour the veggie mixture onto the baking sheet and arrange in a single layer. Bake for 25 to 30 minutes, stirring once, until tender and lightly brown. If the veggies are tender but not brown, place them under the broiler on high for 30 to 45 seconds.

3. **Assemble the tacos.** Scoop the filling into the two tortillas. Drizzle with lime juice, then top with the salsa and any additional toppings (if using). Serve immediately.

Spicy Lentil Lettuce Wrap

To me, this is the perfect lunch. It's healthy and all-natural, but it's also delicious. It's filling, but it won't leave you feeling weighed down. If you like it spicy, go ahead and add more hot sauce!

Serves 1

Prep time: 10 minutes

1 small avocado

1 carrot

¼ teaspoon lemon juice

1 (15-ounce) can lentils

¼ teaspoon ground cumin

¼ teaspoon
   smoked paprika

½ teaspoon favorite
   hot sauce, plus more
   for topping

2 large Boston
   lettuce leaves

Salt

Black pepper

1. **Prepare the filling.** Carefully halve, pit, and peel the avocado (see page 19). Transfer the fruit to a small bowl and mash with the back of a fork. Grate the carrot using a box grater and add it to the bowl. Add the lemon juice and mix well.

2. **Season the lentils.** Measure out 1 cup of lentils (refrigerate the rest for another use). Add them to another small bowl, then mix with the cumin, paprika, and hot sauce. Taste and add more hot sauce, as desired.

3. **Build the wraps.** Place both leaves of lettuce on your plate. Spoon in the lentils, half into each leaf. Top with the avocado mixture, then sprinkle with salt and pepper. Drizzle with hot sauce and enjoy.

Did You Know? Boston and butter lettuce are similar in size and texture and can easily be substituted for each other. Bibb lettuce is also similar, but will hold less filling.

Big Barbecue Tempeh Salad

Serves 1
Prep time: 10 minutes
Cook time: 15 minutes

For the tempeh

1 (4-ounce) block tempeh

1 tablespoon olive oil

¼ cup vegan barbe-
cue sauce

For the salad

2 cups chopped lettuce
of choice

6 grape tomatoes

2 mini sweet peppers
(any color)

1 small carrot

2 to 3 tablespoons vegan
ranch or favorite creamy
dressing

Salt

Black pepper

If you haven't spent a lot of time cooking with tempeh, this is a great dish to start with. Tempeh is affordable and easy to find in many super-markets. Just be sure to always steam, simmer, or sauté the tempeh before adding sauces or seasonings; otherwise, it can have a slightly bitter taste.

1. **Cook the tempeh.** Halve the tempeh. Wrap up one half and refrigerate it for later. Cut the remaining half into bite-size pieces. In a small pan over medium-high heat, heat the oil until it shimmers. Add the tempeh and cook, stirring, for 6 to 7 minutes, until it is lightly golden brown. Stir in the barbecue sauce and cook for 2 to 3 minutes, then remove from the heat.

2. **Make the salad.** Add the lettuce to a serving bowl. Halve the tomatoes and add to the bowl. Cut the peppers and carrots into thin circles and add to the bowl. Mix everything to combine. Top with the dressing, tempeh, and salt and pepper to taste, then serve.

Did You Know? Tempeh, like tofu, is made from soybeans, but the beans maintain their shape and are fermented and bound together into a block.

Easy Mac 'n' Cheesy

5 INGREDIENT
30-MINUTE
ONE-POT

Serves 1
Prep time: 5 minute
Cook time: 20 minutes

1 cup dried small
shell pasta

½ cup vegan cheddar
cheese shreds

¼ cup unsweetened
nondairy milk

½ teaspoon
yellow mustard

⅛ teaspoon vegan
Worcestershire sauce

Salt

Black pepper

The ultimate comfort food—for one! You can throw this together after school or after practice with very little effort. The secret ingredient to making the cheese sauce extra creamy is adding back in some of the cooking liquid. I like mine really creamy, so I usually use 2 to 3 tablespoons.

1. **Cook the pasta.** Bring a medium saucepan of salted water to a boil over high heat. Add the pasta and cook according to package instructions until tender, usually about 10 minutes. Drain, reserving the cooking liquid, and return to the pot over low heat.

2. **Make the sauce.** Add the cheese and milk. Stir until the cheese is melted. Add the mustard and Worcestershire sauce. Add the cooking liquid, 1 to 2 teaspoons at a time, stirring to incorporate it before adding more. Keep this up until the sauce is as creamy as you'd like.

3. **Adjust the seasonings.** Taste, then add salt and pepper as needed. Because you salted the cooking water and vegan cheese can be salty, you may only need to add pepper. Enjoy!

Lemon-Butter Spaghetti Squash

Serves 1
Prep time: 5 minutes
Cook time: 50 minutes

Nonstick spray
1 small spaghetti squash
1 tablespoon vegan butter
2 teaspoons lemon juice
½ teaspoon salt
¼ to ½ teaspoon
   garlic powder
Red pepper flakes, for
   topping (optional)

This is like a hearty bowl of pasta except . . . it's squash! This makes for a flavorful yet light meal that won't weigh you down.

1. **Prepare the squash.** Preheat the oven to 400°F. Lightly coat a baking sheet with nonstick spray. Halve the squash lengthwise, from stem to base. (Be very careful and ask for help if you need it!) Use a spoon to scoop out the seeds and pulpy center from the squash.

2. **Bake.** Place the two squash halves, cut-side down, on the prepared baking sheet. Bake for 40 to 50 minutes, until it's tender when you press it with the back of a spoon. Remove the squash from the oven, use tongs to flip it over, and let it cool for 2 to 3 minutes.

3. **Season and serve.** Use a spoon or fork to scrape out the "spaghetti" strands from the squash. Keep going until you're nearly to the inside of the rind. Transfer them to a serving bowl. Add the butter, lemon juice, salt, and garlic powder to the bowl, stirring to coat the squash evenly. Sprinkle with red pepper flakes (if using) and enjoy!

Change It Up: Try doubling this recipe and serving it as a side dish, perhaps with the Italian Meat Loaf (page 92)!

Roasted Beet Salad

Serves 1
Prep time: 15 minutes
Cook time: 15 minutes

For the beets

2 beets
1 teaspoon olive oil
⅛ teaspoon salt

For the salad

1½ cups chopped spinach
1/4 cup frozen edamame, thawed
2 tablespoons slivered almonds
2 tablespoons dried sweetened cranberries
Salt
Black pepper
Balsamic vinaigrette, for serving

I love beets and will eat them every chance I get. I know some people aren't as fond of them, but I suspect those people haven't tried roasting them with a little oil and salt. It brings out their natural sweetness! If you don't like raw spinach, use your favorite salad greens.

1. **Prep the beets.** Preheat the oven to 400°F. Line a baking sheet with parchment paper. Trim the stem and root end from the beets, then use a vegetable peeler to carefully remove the skin. Cut the beets into ¼-inch-thick slices, then toss them in a bowl with the oil.

2. **Roast the beets.** On the prepared baking sheet, arrange the beets in a single layer. Sprinkle with the salt. Bake for 10 to 15 minutes, until tender. Remove from the oven and let cool. Once cooled enough to touch, cut the slices into quarters.

3. **Build the salad.** In a large bowl, mix the spinach, edamame, almonds, cranberries, and beets. Add salt and pepper as desired, then drizzle with vinaigrette. Enjoy!

Did You Know? What we call beets are actually the root of the beet plant. They are also called "beetroots." Red beets are the most common, but they also come in a golden variety.

Super Quick Sesame Soba Noodles

30-MINUTE
NUT-FREE
ONE-POT

Serves 1
Prep time: 5 minutes
Cook time: 20 minutes

4 ounces dried
   soba noodles

1 tablespoon rice vinegar

2 tablespoons soy sauce

2 teaspoons sesame oil

½ teaspoon ground ginger

¼ teaspoon garlic powder

¼ teaspoon sugar

1 to 2 scallions, green
   parts only, thinly sliced
   (optional)

1 to 2 teaspoons toasted
   sesame seeds (optional)

Soba is the Japanese word for "buckwheat," and soba noodles are made from buckwheat flour! They can be found in the international food aisle at most grocery stores or at Asian markets.

1. **Cook the soba noodles.** Bring a medium pot of water to a boil over high heat. Add the soba noodles and cook according to package instructions until tender, usually about 5 minutes. Drain and rinse the noodles well with cold water and set aside.

2. **Mix the sauce.** Place the pot over medium-low heat. Whisk together the vinegar, soy sauce, sesame oil, ginger, garlic powder, and sugar until combined. Add the noodles back to the pot and toss until evenly coated. Let sit over the heat for 1 to 2 minutes, until heated through. Top with the scallions (if using) and sesame seeds (if using) and enjoy!

Change It Up: Soba noodles are generally prepared with scallions and garlic, but if you want to add more veggies, try the kind you can microwave in the bag. Then simply add them to the sauce in step 2 along with the noodles!

Spaghetti Aglio e Olio

5 INGREDIENT
30-MINUTE
NUT-FREE
SOY-FREE

Serves 1
Prep time: 5 minutes
Cook time: 20 minutes

2 ounces dried spaghetti

1 tablespoon olive oil

1 teaspoon minced garlic

⅛ teaspoon red pepper
flakes, or more
as desired

1 teaspoon chopped fresh
parsley (optional)

1 teaspoon nutritional
yeast (optional)

This is what I make when I'm craving a quick bowl of pasta, and it always hits the spot. Olive oil, garlic, and red pepper flakes are a delicious combo—perfect on their own if you don't have fresh parsley or nutritional yeast (aka "nooch") on hand.

1. **Cook the pasta.** In a medium saucepan, bring 5 cups of salted water to a boil. Cook the spaghetti per package instructions, minus 1 minute, so the pasta is still a little firm. When it's done, strain the pasta into a colander over a bowl or measuring cup and set aside ½ cup of the cooking liquid.

2. **Make the sauce.** While the pasta is cooking, in a large skillet over medium-high heat, heat the oil until it shimmers. Add the garlic and red pepper flakes. Cook, stirring almost continuously, for 3 to 4 minutes, until the garlic is lightly golden brown. Remove the saucepan from the heat until the pasta is done.

3. **Combine the pasta and sauce.** Add the cooked spaghetti to the pan, along with ¼ cup of the reserved cooking liquid. Stir until the spaghetti is completely coated, adding another 2 to 3 tablespoons of cooking liquid if the pasta is too dry. Serve topped with parsley (if using) and nutritional yeast (if using) for a salty, cheesy flavor!

Did You Know? *Aglio e olio* means "olive oil and garlic" in Italian! This recipe originated in Naples but has become a staple across Italy and much of the world.

Veggie Noodle Casserole, page 88

Meals for Many

Pizza Supreme

ONE-POT

Serves 4

Prep time: 20 minutes,
plus 40 minutes to rest

Cook time: 25 minutes

For the crust

½ cup warm water

½ teaspoon apple
cider vinegar

1 tablespoon olive oil

1½ cups all-purpose flour

2 teaspoons Italian
seasoning mix

1 teaspoon baking powder

½ teaspoon salt

⅛ teaspoon baking soda

For the pizza

1 small bell pepper
(any color)

½ sweet onion

1 cup pizza sauce, plus
more to taste

½ cup vegan pepperoni or
sliced sausage

½ cup sliced mushrooms

1 to 1½ cups vegan
mozzarella
cheese shreds

Red pepper flakes,
for topping

This is a great starter recipe if you haven't made your own dough before. Once you're comfortable making the dough, try experimenting with the veggies!

1. **Make the dough.** In a large bowl, whisk together the water, vinegar, and oil. In a separate bowl, stir together the flour, Italian seasoning, baking powder, salt, and baking soda. Transfer this mixture to the wet ingredients and stir together.

2. **Knead.** In the bowl, knead the dough with your hands for 3 to 4 minutes, until it forms a smooth ball. If it's too dry, add another tablespoon of warm water. Cover the bowl with a towel and let the dough rest for 30 to 40 minutes.

3. **Prepare the veggies.** Preheat the oven to 425°F. Line a baking sheet with parchment paper. Cut the bell pepper and onion into very thin slices.

4. **Shape the dough.** Coat your hands with a little oil and use them to stretch the dough into a circle or rectangle. Lay it on the prepared baking sheet in one thin, even layer about ¼-inch thick. This will give you a thin crust, but you can make it thicker if you like.

5. **Make the pizza.** Spread ⅔ cup of the pizza sauce evenly over the crust, going almost all the way to the outer edge. Sprinkle the pepper, onion, pepperoni, and mushrooms evenly over the sauce. Add the remaining ⅓ cup of sauce (or more to taste), followed by the cheese.

6. **Bake.** Bake for 18 to 20 minutes, until the crust is crispy and the cheese is melted. Garnish with red pepper flakes and enjoy!

Baked Ziti

Serves 6
Prep time: 15 minutes
Cook time: 30 minutes

4 cups dried ziti or
  similar pasta

1 tablespoon olive oil

1 small sweet onion

2 red or orange
  bell peppers

½ teaspoon minced garlic

2 precooked vegan Italian
  sausage links

1 (25-ounce) jar favorite
  pasta sauce

1 (14.5-ounce) can
  fire-roasted diced
  tomatoes

¼ teaspoon red pepper
  flakes, or more

1 teaspoon Italian
  seasoning

1 cup vegan mozzarella
  cheese shreds

Salt

Black pepper

This popular Italian American dish was my first foray into "intuitive cooking," or cooking with one's intuition. For me, this was fun because I could explore different ingredients that were interesting. Try it!

1. **Precook the pasta.** Preheat the oven to 375°F. Cook the pasta in salted water per package instructions, minus 2 minutes. Reserve ¾ cup of the cooking liquid, then drain the pasta and return to the pot.

2. **Prepare the veggies and sausage.** While the pasta is cooking, cut the onion and peppers into large dice. In a medium skillet over medium-high heat, heat the oil until it shimmers. Add the peppers, onion, and garlic and cook, stirring frequently, for 3 to 4 minutes. Remove from the heat and set aside. Cut the sausages into thin slices. Some brands may need to be browned, which should be done at this step.

3. **Combine.** Add the cooked vegetables, sauce, tomatoes with their juices, sausages, red pepper flakes, Italian seasoning, and reserved cooking liquid to the pasta. Stir until well combined.

4. **Bake.** Transfer the pasta mixture into a 2.5-quart (or larger) baking dish. Sprinkle the cheese over the top, along with salt and pepper, then cover with aluminum foil. Bake for 20 to 30 minutes, until bubbling and the cheese is melted. Let sit for 5 minutes before serving.

Decadent Fettuccine Alfredo

Serves 4

Prep time: 15 minutes,
plus 4 hours to
soak cashews

Cook time: 30 minutes

8 ounces dried fettuc-
cine pasta

2 cups raw cashews,
soaked for 4 hours
and rinsed

⅓ cup nutritional yeast

1 ½ to 2 cups unsweet-
ened cashew milk

1 tablespoon cornstarch

¾ teaspoon salt

½ teaspoon garlic powder

¼ teaspoon onion powder

1 cup vegan mozzarella
cheese shreds

1 cup frozen peas

Black pepper

Alfredo sauce is often served with fettuccine,
but I will admit that I also really enjoy this sauce
served with smaller pastas, like penne, that have
little pockets. You get more sauce with each bite!

1. **Cook the pasta.** Bring a large pot of salted water to
   a boil over high heat. Add the pasta and cook according to package instructions until tender, usually
   about 12 minutes. Drain and set aside.

2. **Blend the sauce.** Meanwhile, combine the
   cashews, nutritional yeast, milk, cornstarch, salt,
   garlic powder, and onion powder in a blender. Blend
   until smooth.

3. **Heat the sauce.** Using a rubber spatula, transfer
   the sauce to a small saucepan over medium heat. Stir
   in the cheese and peas and bring to a simmer. Turn
   off the heat, cover, and let sit for 2 to 3 minutes, until
   heated through.

4. **Combine.** Stir the cooked pasta into the sauce.
   Serve topped with a little salt and pepper.

Garlicky-Lemon Broccoli Noodles

Serves 4
Prep time: 15 minutes
Cook time: 20 minutes

2 heads broccoli

1 lemon

8 ounces dried
   cellentani pasta

3 tablespoons olive oil

1½ teaspoons
   minced garlic

1 teaspoon salt

¼ teaspoon black pepper

¼ cup chopped fresh
   parsley, for topping

2 teaspoons red pepper
   flakes, for topping

I love garlic's earthy flavor and warm spiciness. It also goes really well with the tartness of fresh lemon juice and the green flavor of broccoli.

1. **Prep the veggies.** Cut the broccoli into small florets and measure out 4 cups. With your palm, roll the lemon back and forth on a cutting board to loosen the juices. Use a zester to zest the lemon into a small bowl. Halve the lemon, then squeeze out 2 tablespoons of juice and add it to the zest.

2. **Cook the pasta.** Bring a large pot of salted water to a boil over high heat. Add the pasta and cook according to package instructions, minus 1 minute. When there are 2 minutes left in the cooking time, add the broccoli. Drain the pasta and broccoli into a colander and leave in the sink.

3. **Combine.** Return the pot to the stovetop and heat the oil over medium-high heat until it shimmers. Add the garlic and cook, stirring often, for 1 to 2 minutes. Add the pasta, broccoli, lemon juice and zest, salt, and pepper. Stir, remove from the heat, cover, and let sit for 2 to 3 minutes. Serve topped with parsley and red pepper flakes.

Ingredient Info: If you aren't familiar with cellentani pasta's fun corkscrew shape, you should be! Because it's a relatively short pasta, it's good for pairing with bite-size pieces of vegetables.

Spaghetti with Creamy Tomato-Basil Sauce

Serves 4

Prep time: 15 minutes, plus 4 hours to soak cashews

Cook time: 25 minutes

8 ounces dried spaghetti pasta

3 large ripe tomatoes, quartered and cored

1 cup raw cashews, soaked for 4 hours and rinsed

½ cup unsweetened nondairy milk

1 cup fresh basil leaves, divided

2 tablespoons olive oil

1½ teaspoons minced garlic

½ small sweet onion, diced

¾ teaspoon salt

¼ teaspoon black pepper

Every spring I plant tomatoes and basil in my garden with visions of this simple dish. Even if your basil and tomatoes come from the store, it will be just as delicious—just be sure your tomatoes are very ripe.

1. **Boil the pasta.** Bring a large pot of salted water to a boil over high heat. Add the pasta and cook according to package instructions, minus 2 minutes. Reserve 1 cup of cooking liquid, then drain.

2. **Blend the sauce.** Combine the tomatoes, cashews, milk, and ½ cup of basil in a blender. Blend until smooth.

3. **Cook the sauce.** In a large skillet over medium heat, heat the oil until it shimmers. Add the garlic and cook, stirring, for 1 minute. Add the onion and cook for 2 to 3 minutes, until fragrant. Use a rubber spatula to add the sauce from the blender. Add the salt and pepper. Increase the heat to high. Bring to a boil, then reduce the heat to low. Cover and simmer, stirring occasionally, for 5 to 6 minutes. Taste and add salt and pepper as needed.

4. **Combine.** Add the pasta to the sauce. Stir in the reserved cooking liquid, 2 to 3 tablespoons at a time, as needed to make things creamy. Simmer uncovered for another 2 to 3 minutes. Serve topped with the remaining basil leaves.

Chili Mac

30-MINUTE
ONE-POT

Serves 4
Prep time: 5 minutes
Cook time: 25 minutes

2 teaspoons salt, divided

3 cups dried elbow pasta

1 (15-ounce) can black
  beans, drained
  and rinsed

1 (14-ounce) can diced
  tomatoes

1 cup frozen corn

2 teaspoons ground cumin

1 teaspoon garlic powder

½ teaspoon onion powder

½ teaspoon chili powder
  (or more)

2½ cups vegan cheddar
  cheese shreds

Black pepper

Cheesy, gooey mac 'n' cheese with all the flavor of chili! This makes a hearty meal for cold days when you're craving some extra spice.

1. **Cook the pasta.** Add 1 teaspoon of salt to a medium pot of water and bring to a boil over high heat. Add the pasta and cook according to package instructions, minus 1 minute. Reserve ½ cup of cooking liquid, then drain in a colander. Stir and set aside.

2. **Prepare the sauce.** Place the pot over medium heat. Pour in the beans, tomatoes and their juices, corn, cumin, remaining 1 teaspoon salt, garlic powder, onion powder, chili powder, and cheese. Stir in ¼ cup of the reserved cooking liquid and bring to a simmer. Reduce heat to low. Simmer, uncovered, for 3 to 4 minutes, until the cheese is melty.

3. **Combine.** Stir the pasta into the sauce. Simmer for 2 minutes, until everything is warm. Stir in the remaining cooking liquid as needed for consistency. Taste and add more salt, pepper, and chili powder, as needed. Serve.

> **Ingredient Info:** Whenever you're cooking pasta, reserve a bit of the cooking liquid—it's very useful for thickening your sauce.

"Cheesy" Lasagna

Serves 6
Prep time: 20 minutes
Cook time: 35 minutes

For the tofu ricotta

1 (14-ounce) block firm
tofu, drained and
pressed for 10 minutes

⅓ cup nutritional yeast

¼ cup unsweetened
nondairy milk

1 tablespoon olive oil

2 tablespoons Italian
seasoning

1 teaspoon salt

¼ teaspoon black pepper

For the lasagna

1 (24-ounce) jar
plus 1 (14-ounce)
jar tomato-basil
pasta sauce

10 to 12 no-boil
lasagna noodles

2 cups vegan mozzarella
cheese shreds

Salt (optional)

Black pepper (optional)

Oregano and red pepper
flakes, for topping

This lasagna recipe is intended to be a starting point for your culinary adventure. Cheesy lasagna is delicious, but there are so many ingredients to experiment with—onions, peppers, sautéed kale, or precooked vegan Italian sausage or chicken. Try layering in whatever you like! Just keep in mind that when you start adding in additional ingredients, you'll want to upgrade to a larger dish to accommodate them, such as a 9-by-13-inch baking dish.

1. **Make the tofu ricotta.** Preheat the oven to 425°F. In a food processor, combine the tofu, nutritional yeast, milk, oil, Italian seasoning, salt, and pepper. Pulse until mixed but not mushy. Taste and adjust the seasonings as needed. Set aside.

2. **Assemble the lasagna.** Spread 2 tablespoons of sauce over the bottom of a 7-by-11-inch baking dish. Add a single layer of noodles (a little overlap is okay), followed by half of the tofu ricotta. Use the back of a spoon to spread it evenly. Sprinkle 1 cup of cheese over the ricotta, then top that with about a third of the remaining sauce. Repeat with another layer of noodles, the remaining half of ricotta, and another third of sauce. Top with a final layer of noodles, the rest of the sauce, and the remaining 1 cup of cheese. Sprinkle with a little salt and pepper (if using), then with oregano and red pepper flakes.

3. **Bake.** Cover the pan with aluminum foil and bake for 25 minutes. Remove the foil and bake for another 5 to 10 minutes, until the cheese is melted. Enjoy!

Ingredient Info: When using oven-ready lasagna noodles, be sure to add a little more sauce or other liquid than you normally would. You can also serve a little extra sauce (warmed!) on the side.

Kitchen Cure: You can make the tofu ricotta one to two days in advance. Store in an airtight container in the fridge.

Veggie Noodle Casserole

Serves 6
Prep time: 20 minutes
Cook time: 20 minutes

1 large head broccoli

3 carrots

3½ cups dried
    pinwheel pasta

1 cup frozen peas

2 tablespoons
    vegan butter

2 tablespoons
    all-purpose flour

2½ cups unsweetened
    nondairy milk

½ teaspoon garlic powder

½ teaspoon salt

¼ teaspoon black pepper

2 cups vegan cheddar
    cheese shreds

½ cup panko
    bread crumbs

Casseroles can seem difficult to veganize because many recipes call for cans of "cream of something" soup. Step 3 of this recipe gives you an easy way around that!

1. **Prepare the veggies.** Preheat the oven to 350°F. Cut the broccoli into florets (about 3½ cups). Slice the carrots into thin coins.

2. **Cook the pasta.** Bring a large pot of salted water to a boil over high heat. Add the pasta and cook for 4 minutes, stirring occasionally. Stir in the broccoli, carrots, and peas. Bring back to a boil and cook for 2 minutes. Drain and pour into a 2.5-quart baking dish.

3. **Make the sauce.** Return the pot to medium-high heat. Melt the butter, then whisk in the flour. While whisking constantly, let bubble for about 1 minute. As you continue whisking, add the milk ½ cup at a time. Whisk until smooth each time before adding more milk. Stir in the garlic powder, salt, and pepper. Reduce the heat to low and stir in the cheese. Cook for 1 to 2 minutes, until the cheese melts.

4. **Bake.** Pour the sauce over the pasta and veggies, stir, then top with the bread crumbs. Cover with aluminum foil and bake for 15 minutes. Remove the foil and bake for 5 minutes more. If the crumbs haven't browned, place the casserole under the broiler on high for 30 to 45 seconds. Enjoy!

Butternut Squash and Quinoa Casserole

Serves 6
Prep time: 15 minutes
Cook time: 35 minutes

Nonstick spray

1 cup quinoa, rinsed
   and drained

2 cups vegetable broth

2 (10-ounce) bags frozen
   butternut squash cubes
   (4 cups)

1 lime

2 to 3 chipotle peppers
   in adobo sauce, plus
   1 teaspoon sauce

1 cup frozen corn

1 (15-ounce) can black
   beans, drained
   and rinsed

1 teaspoon ground cumin

1 teaspoon garlic powder

½ teaspoon salt

¼ teaspoon black pepper

2 cups vegan cheddar
   cheese shreds, divided

Black beans, lime, adobo, and cumin are flavors often paired with sweet potato, but they go just as well with butternut squash!

1. **Cook the quinoa and squash.** Preheat the oven to 350°F. Lightly coat a 2.5-quart baking dish with nonstick spray. Combine the quinoa and broth in a medium saucepan over high heat. Bring to a boil, then reduce the heat to low. Simmer, covered, for 15 minutes, until the liquid has been absorbed. Meanwhile, microwave the squash per package instructions, usually 5 to 10 minutes, then drain. In the prepared baking dish, combine the quinoa and squash.

2. **Prep the lime and peppers.** Zest the lime, then juice it. Measure out 1 tablespoon of juice and add it to the baking dish. Dice the peppers and add them to the baking dish along with the sauce.

3. **Bake.** Stir in the corn, beans, cumin, garlic powder, salt, pepper, and 1 cup of cheese. Top with the remaining 1 cup of cheese. Cover with aluminum foil and bake for 15 minutes. Remove the foil and bake for 5 minutes more, until the cheese melts.

Change It Up: Have some extra time and craving a sweet, roasted flavor? Roast the butternut instead of microwaving it. (See Chipotle Butternut Wrap on page 60 for roasting instructions.)

Loaded Cauliflower Casserole

Serves 6
Prep time: 15 minutes
Cook time: 40 minutes

For the cauliflower

2 heads cauliflower

2 tablespoons olive oil

1 teaspoon salt

¼ teaspoon black pepper

For the casserole

2 tablespoons
   vegan butter

2 tablespoons
   all-purpose flour

1 cup unsweetened
   nondairy milk

½ teaspoon salt

¼ teaspoon black pepper

2 cups shredded vegan
   cheddar cheese, divided

½ cup vegan sour cream

2 cups frozen peas

6 to 8 slices vegan bacon,
   diced (1 cup)

2 to 3 scallions, green
   parts only, sliced
   (optional)

This casserole is like a loaded baked potato *except* with cauliflower instead of potatoes. The sour cream sauce is my favorite part!

1. **Roast the cauliflower.** Preheat the oven to 375°F. Cut the cauliflower into florets and place on a baking sheet. Drizzle with the oil, then sprinkle with the salt and pepper. Stir and arrange in a single layer. Bake for 25 minutes, stirring once halfway through.

2. **Make the sauce.** Meanwhile, in a medium saucepan over medium-high heat, melt the butter. Whisk in the flour. Whisking constantly, let bubble for about 1 minute. Slowly whisk in the milk, making sure it's smooth before adding more. Stir in the salt and pepper. Reduce the heat to low and stir in 1 cup of cheese. Cook for 1 to 2 minutes, until the cheese melts. Remove from the heat, then stir in the sour cream. Taste and add more salt, pepper, and sour cream as needed.

3. **Bake.** In a 2.5-quart baking dish, stir together the cauliflower, peas, and sauce. Top with the remaining cheese, then cover with aluminum foil. Bake for 10 minutes, then remove the foil. Sprinkle the bacon across the top, then bake for 5 minutes followed by 30 to 45 seconds under the broiler. Top with scallions before serving (if using).

Chile-Garlic Tempeh Stir-Fry

Serves 4
Prep time: 20 minutes
Cook time: 25 minutes

For the sauce

1 tablespoon cornstarch

2 tablespoons cold water

¼ cup veggie broth

3 tablespoons soy sauce

1 to 2 tablespoons chile-garlic sauce

2 to 3 tablespoons real maple syrup

1 tablespoon olive oil

1 teaspoon lime juice

½ teaspoon ground ginger

½ teaspoon red pepper flakes

For the stir-fry

1 (8-ounce) package tempeh

2 tablespoons olive oil

1 (12-ounce) bag frozen stir-fry vegetables

2 cups cooked rice, for serving

Frozen vegetables are a great hack for when you want to focus your energy on the sauce! Start with 2 tablespoons of the chile sauce and use an equal amount of maple syrup for balance.

1. **Mix the sauce.** In a medium bowl, whisk together the cornstarch and water. Whisk in the broth, soy sauce, chile sauce, maple syrup, oil, lime juice, ginger, and red pepper flakes. Set aside.

2. **Cook the tempeh.** Cut the tempeh into ¼-inch cubes. In a large skillet over medium-high heat, heat the oil until it shimmers. Add the tempeh and cook, flipping occasionally, for 6 to 8 minutes, until lightly browned all over. Pour half of the sauce into the pan, stirring to coat. Remove from the pan and set aside.

3. **Cook the veggies.** Add the veggies and cook per package instructions (this usually includes a small amount of water and simmering for 8 to 10 minutes). Add the tempeh and remaining sauce to the pan and simmer for 4 to 5 minutes, stirring occasionally. Add water, 1 to 2 tablespoons at a time, if the sauce gets too thick. Serve hot over the rice.

Kitchen Cure: There are quite a few brands of precooked rice that come in pouches and just need to be microwaved.

Italian Meat Loaf

NUT-FREE
ONE-POT

Serves 6
Prep time: 10 minutes
Cook time: 1 hour

1 green bell pepper

1 small sweet onion

1 pound meatless
    ground beef

1 cup panko bread crumbs

1 tablespoon vegan
    Worcestershire sauce

1 tablespoon
    balsamic vinegar

1 tablespoon Italian
    seasoning

½ teaspoon salt

¼ teaspoon black pepper

½ cup ketchup

When I became vegan, meat loaf was the one of the meals I missed most. But luckily with all the "practically real" mock meats in stores now, it's back! If you can, try to use a high-quality brand, such as Beyond or Impossible. They have a lot of fat in them that helps hold the loaf together and keeps it from drying out.

1. **Chop the veggies.** Preheat the oven to 350°F. Dice the bell pepper and onion.

2. **Mix the ingredients.** In a large bowl, combine the ground beef, bell pepper, onion, bread crumbs, Worcestershire sauce, vinegar, Italian seasoning, salt, and pepper. Mix with your hands or a large spoon until well combined.

3. **Form the loaf.** Transfer the mixture to a loaf pan. Spread the ketchup evenly across the top.

4. **Bake.** Bake for about 1 hour, until firm and just slightly pink at the center. Let rest for about 5 minutes before slicing and serving.

Change It Up: Try serving the meat loaf with Mashed Potatoes and Gravy (page 50) and your favorite green veggie.

Kitchen Cure: If you don't have a loaf pan, put the mixture on a baking sheet and, using your hands, form it into a loaf shape with a mostly flat top.

Baking Sheet Fajitas

Serves 4 to 6
Prep time: 15 minutes
Cook time: 25 minutes

Nonstick spray

1 (14-ounce) block firm or
extra-firm tofu, drained
and pressed for at least
15 minutes

2 bell peppers (any color)

1 sweet onion

1 sweet potato

¼ cup lime juice

2 tablespoons soy sauce

1 tablespoon olive oil

1 teaspoon ground cumin

1 teaspoon garlic powder

½ teaspoon chili powder
(or more)

¼ teaspoon black pepper

8 to 10 fajita-size corn or
flour tortillas

Sliced avocado, vegan
sour cream, chopped
fresh cilantro, and salsa,
for topping (optional)

I'm a big fan of handheld foods, especially those that are Mexican-inspired. If you don't like peppers or onions, use the veggies you do like. Butternut squash, zucchini, and summer squash would be great!

1. **Prepare the tofu and veggies.** Preheat the oven to 425°F. Lightly coat a baking sheet with nonstick spray. Cut the tofu into ½- to ¾-inch cubes. Cut the bell peppers, onion, and sweet potato into pieces similar in size to the tofu.

2. **Mix the marinade.** In a large bowl, whisk together the lime juice, soy sauce, oil, cumin, garlic powder, chili powder, and black pepper. Toss with the tofu and veggies, then spread in a single layer on the prepared baking sheet.

3. **Bake the fajitas.** Bake for 15 minutes, then stir well using tongs. Bake for another 10 minutes, until the veggies are tender and the tofu is golden brown.

4. **Build the fajitas.** Place the tortillas on plates and use the tongs to fill each evenly. Add toppings (if using) and serve.

Change It Up: Serve with vegetarian refried beans (canned varieties are widely available) and a side salad.

Cowboy Beans and Rice

NUT-FREE
ONE-POT

Serves 4
Prep time: 20 minutes
Cook time: 25 minutes

1¼ cups water

⅓ cup packed brown sugar

3 tablespoons
    tomato paste

2 tablespoons
    yellow mustard

1 tablespoon cornstarch

1 teaspoon garlic powder

1 teaspoon
    smoked paprika

1 teaspoon salt

½ teaspoon chili powder
    (or more)

1 (15-ounce) can pinto
    beans, drained
    and rinsed

1 (15-ounce) can kidney
    beans, drained
    and rinsed

1 red bell pepper, diced

6 to 8 slices Baked
    Tofu Bacon (page 14),
    thinly sliced

2 to 3 cups cooked rice,
    for serving

Cowboy beans are similar to baked beans but with a Southwestern twist (chili powder!) and meat (usually). You could definitely use vegan ground beef, but I thought bacon would be a delicious option, too.

1. **Combine the ingredients.** Heat a medium sauce-pan over high heat. Add the water, brown sugar, tomato paste, mustard, cornstarch, garlic powder, paprika, salt, and chili powder. Stir until completely combined. Add the beans and bell pepper.

2. **Simmer.** Bring to a boil, then reduce the heat to low. Cover and simmer for 8 to 10 minutes, stirring occasionally. If the mixture gets too thick, add water, 2 to 3 tablespoons at a time. Remove from the heat.

3. **Add the bacon.** Stir the bacon into the beans. Let sit, uncovered, for 1 to 2 minutes. Taste and add more chili powder and salt as needed. Serve over rice.

Ingredient Info: If you're using a store-bought vegan bacon for this recipe, be sure to cook it per package instructions before adding it to the beans.

Baked Teriyaki Tofu with Asparagus

Serves 4
Prep time: 20 minutes
Cook time: 30 minutes

1 (14-ounce) block firm
   tofu, drained and
   pressed for 20 minutes

Nonstick spray

¼ cup soy sauce

3 tablespoons
   brown sugar

⅓ cup vegetable broth

1 teaspoon ground ginger

½ teaspoon garlic powder

1 tablespoon cornstarch

2 tablespoons cold water

1 bunch asparagus, woody
   stems trimmed

2 tablespoons olive oil

½ teaspoon salt

¼ teaspoon black pepper

Roasted asparagus is delicious and pairs well with sweet teriyaki sauce. If you want to make this meal heartier, serve it with brown rice or quinoa.

1. **Bake the tofu.** Preheat the oven to 375°F. Line a baking sheet with parchment paper. Cut the tofu into ½- to ¾-inch cubes. Place in a single layer on the prepared baking sheet. Spritz with nonstick spray and bake for 20 minutes. Flip, then spritz again. Bake for 15 minutes, then remove. Turn off the oven and turn the broiler on low.

2. **Make the sauce.** In a medium skillet over high heat, combine the soy sauce, brown sugar, broth, ginger, and garlic powder. Bring to a boil, then reduce the heat to low. In a small bowl, stir together the cornstarch and water, then slowly stir it into the sauce. Stir in the tofu and cover. Simmer for 6 to 8 minutes.

3. **Roast the asparagus.** Meanwhile, line the baking sheet with clean parchment paper. Arrange the asparagus on it in a single layer. Drizzle with the oil, then top with the salt and pepper. Broil for 6 to 8 minutes, turning once. Watch so it doesn't burn! Toss the asparagus and tofu together in a bowl and serve.

Ingredient Info: Hold one piece of asparagus by each end. Bend, and where it snaps is the "natural breaking point" where the stem turns woody. Now you know where to trim the rest!

Spicy Hawaiian-Inspired Chickpea Burgers

Serves 4
Prep time: 15 minutes, plus 2 hours to chill
Cook time: 45 minutes

1 tablespoon chia seeds
3 tablespoons water
½ red bell pepper
½ sweet onion
1 (15-ounce) can chick-peas, rinsed and drained
1 (12-ounce) can pine-apple rings packed in juice
¾ cup bread crumbs
1 tablespoon teriyaki sauce
½ teaspoon red pepper flakes
½ teaspoon garlic powder
½ teaspoon salt
⅛ teaspoon black pepper
Nonstick spray
4 slices of vegan cheese
4 hamburger buns
Vegan mayo
Sriracha, for topping

These burgers are the perfect combination of sweet 'n' spicy. The teriyaki and pineapple give the patties just a hint of sweet. I love the flavor of pineapple and sriracha—they were made for each other!

1. **Make the chia "egg."** In a small bowl, mix the chia seeds and water and set aside.

2. **Make the burger mix.** Cut the bell pepper and onion into large chunks, then transfer to the food processor. Add the chickpeas, 1 tablespoon of pine-apple juice from the can, the bread crumbs, teriyaki sauce, red pepper flakes, garlic powder, salt, and pepper. Pulse 2 to 3 times, then add the chia egg. Pulse 1 to 2 more times, until combined. You don't want any large pieces to remain, but you also don't want the mixture to be too liquid. Cover and refrig-erate for 1 to 2 hours.

3. **Form and bake.** Preheat the oven to 375°F. Lightly coat a baking sheet with nonstick spray. Use your hands to give the burger mix a quick stir, then separate into four patties. Arrange them in a single later on the baking sheet. Bake for 25 minutes. Spritz with nonstick spray and use a spatula to flip them. Bake for another 20 to 25 minutes, or until cooked through and firm. Add the cheese. Turn off the oven and set the broiler to high. Broil the burgers for 30 to 45 seconds, until the cheese melts (don't let it burn!).

4. **Assemble.** Slather the cut sides of all four buns with mayo, then add the patties to the bottom buns. Top each with 1 to 2 pineapple rings and a small drizzle of sriracha. Enjoy!

Butternut Squash and Kale Orzo

This dish is full of protein and vitamins and is a meal on its own, but it also makes a delicious side dish!

Serves 4 to 6
Prep time: 15 minutes
Cook time: 30 minutes

1 cup dried orzo pasta

1 (12-ounce) bag frozen butternut squash cubes

1 bunch kale

2 tablespoons olive oil

½ teaspoon minced garlic

¼ cup vegetable broth

1 (15-ounce) can chickpeas, rinsed and drained

½ teaspoon salt

¼ teaspoon black pepper

⅛ to ¼ teaspoon red pepper flakes

1. **Cook the past.** Place the pasta in a medium saucepan and add enough water to cover it by 2 to 3 inches. Bring to a boil, then reduce heat to low. Cover and simmer for 7 to 8 minutes, until barely tender. Drain in a fine-mesh colander and set aside.

2. **Microwave the butternut.** Meanwhile, microwave the squash per package instructions, usually 5 to 10 minutes, then drain in the same colander as the pasta.

3. **Cook the kale.** Remove the kale stems and tear the leaves into bite-size pieces. In the same saucepan, over medium heat, heat the oil until it shimmers. Add the garlic and cook for 1 minute, then stir in the kale, broth, and chickpeas. Cover and cook, stirring occasionally, for 5 to 6 minutes, until the kale has wilted. Uncover the pan and add the salt, pepper, and red pepper flakes.

4. **Combine.** Stir in the orzo and squash. Reduce heat to low and cook for 1 to 2 minutes, until the liquid has evaporated and everything is warmed through. Taste and add more salt and pepper, as needed. Enjoy!

Did You Know? *Orzo* is the Italian word for "barley."

Baked Chimichangas

Serves 6
Prep time: 15 minutes
Cook time: 25 minutes

Nonstick spray
1 tablespoon olive oil
1 teaspoon minced garlic
1 bell pepper (any color), diced
1 small onion, diced
1 (15-ounce) can vegetarian refried beans
1 (10-ounce) bag frozen cauliflower rice
1 cup frozen sweet corn
1 cup vegan cheddar cheese shreds
1 cup salsa
1 teaspoon ground cumin
½ teaspoon smoked paprika
½ teaspoon chili powder
½ teaspoon salt
6 large flour tortillas
Vegan sour cream, guacamole, and shredded lettuce, for topping (optional)

Chimichangas are a crispy, deep-fried Tex-Mex burrito. Deep-frying at home can be tricky, so I bake them with a little nonstick spray to crisp them in the oven.

1. **Prep the veggies.** Preheat the oven to 400°F. Lightly coat a baking sheet with nonstick spray. In a medium saucepan over medium-high heat, heat the oil until it shimmers. Add the garlic, bell pepper, and onion. Cook, stirring occasionally, for 3 to 4 minutes.

2. **Make the filling.** Stir in the beans, cauliflower, corn, cheese, salsa, cumin, smoked paprika, chili powder, and salt. Reduce heat to low. Simmer for 6 to 8 minutes, then remove from the heat.

3. **Roll the burritos.** Place the tortillas on a clean surface. Spoon an equal amount of filling into each tortilla, then fold the two sides over the filling and roll up. Transfer, seam-side down, to the prepared baking sheet.

4. **Bake.** Spritz the top of the burritos with the nonstick spray. Bake for about 8 minutes, until lightly browned. Flip them, then spritz again. Turn off the oven and turn the broiler on low. Broil for just 1 minute, until lightly browned and crisp. They are now chimichangas! Cool for 3 to 4 minutes before serving with toppings (if using).

Spicy Red Beans and Rice

Serves 4
Prep time: 20 minutes
Cook time: 40 minutes

2 celery stalks

1 green bell pepper

½ onion

1 tablespoon olive oil

2 (15.5-ounce) cans kidney or red beans, drained (not rinsed)

1½ cups vegetable broth

2 teaspoons dried parsley

1 teaspoon garlic powder

1 teaspoon dried thyme

1 teaspoon salt

½ teaspoon black pepper

¼ teaspoon cayenne pepper (or more)

4 cups cooked white or brown rice, for serving

This is my ode to New Orleans, one of my favorite cities on earth! I was told that New Orleanians eat this dish on Mondays after a weekend of rich meals as a healthy reset to their diet. It's full of veggies and protein—and a bit of spice!

1. **Prep the veggies.** Cut the celery, bell pepper, and onion into small dice. In a large saucepan over medium-high heat, heat the oil until it shimmers. Reduce the heat to medium, add the veggies, and cook, stirring, for 4 to 5 minutes, until just tender.

2. **Add the beans and simmer.** Add the beans, broth, parsley, garlic powder, thyme, salt, pepper, and cayenne. Turn the heat to high and bring to a boil, then reduce heat to low. Simmer, uncovered, for 30 minutes, stirring occasionally. Taste and add more cayenne, salt, and pepper as needed. Add another 3 to 4 tablespoons of broth if you want a soupier consistency.

3. **Plate and serve.** Cool for 1 to 2 minutes, then serve in bowls over the rice.

Ingredient Info: Cayenne peppers are closely related to bell peppers but are much hotter! Start with ¼ teaspoon of cayenne pepper, then add more if you want it spicier when you taste the beans at the end of step 2.

Southwestern Stuffed Zucchini with Avocado Crema

Serves 4
Prep time: 10 minutes
Cook time: 40 minutes

For the zucchini

2 medium zucchini

1 small sweet onion

1 red bell pepper

1 tablespoon olive oil

1 teaspoon minced garlic

1 (15-ounce) can black beans, drained and rinsed

1 (10-ounce) can fire-roasted diced toma- toes with green chiles

½ teaspoon ground cumin

½ teaspoon salt

½ teaspoon chili powder

2 tablespoons water

For the crema

1 avocado

3 to 4 tablespoons unsweetened nondairy milk

2 teaspoons olive oil

½ teaspoon lime juice

¼ teaspoon salt

Develop your intuitive cooking skills with this recipe by playing with the spice level or using a different type of bean.

1. **Hollow out the zucchini.** Preheat the oven to 400°F. Halve each zucchini lengthwise, then scoop out the insides, leaving a ¼-inch outer edge on each side. Transfer them, cut-side up, on a baking sheet.

2. **Make the filling.** Cut the onion and bell pepper into large dice. In a medium skillet over medium heat, heat the olive oil until it shimmers. Add the garlic and cook, stirring, for 1 minute. Add the onion and bell pepper and cook for 2 to 3 minutes. Stir in the beans, tomatoes with their liquid, cumin, salt, chili powder, and water. Reduce heat to low. Cover and simmer for 2 to 3 minutes, until heated through.

3. **Bake.** Spoon equal amounts of the filling into the zucchini halves. Cover loosely with aluminum foil. Bake for 25 to 30 minutes, until the zucchini is soft.

4. **Make the crema.** When the zucchini has about 5 minutes left, carefully halve, pit, and peel the avo- cado (see page 19). Transfer the fruit to a blender. Add the milk (starting with 3 tablespoons), oil, lime juice, and salt. Blend until smooth, adding more milk as needed to make it pourable.

5. **Serve.** Plate the zucchini and drizzle each with the crema right before serving.

Cashew Tofu

Serves 4
Prep time: 30 minutes
Cook time: 17 minutes

For the sauce

⅓ cup soy sauce

⅓ cup water

¼ cup real maple syrup

2 tablespoons rice
   wine vinegar

1 teaspoon ground ginger

½ teaspoon sesame oil

⅛ teaspoon black pepper

For the stir-fry

1 tablespoon sesame oil

2 red bell peppers, cut
   into 2-inch strips

1 small sweet onion, cut
   into 2-inch strips

1 (14-ounce) block
   firm tofu, drained
   and pressed for
   30 minutes and cut into
   bite-size cubes

¾ cup roasted cashews
Cooked rice, for serving
Sesame seeds and sliced
   scallions, for topping
   (optional)

Takeout is great, but sometimes recreating a restaurant dish you love at home is even better. If you want this to be spicy, try mixing in 1 to 2 teaspoons of sriracha during step 1.

1. **Make the sauce.** In a medium bowl, whisk together the soy sauce, water, maple syrup, vinegar, ginger, sesame oil, and pepper.

2. **Cook the veggies.** In a medium skillet over medium-high heat, heat the sesame oil until it shimmers. Add the bell peppers and onion. Cook, stirring occasionally, for 4 to 5 minutes, until crisp-tender.

3. **Add the tofu and sauce.** Stir in the tofu and sauce, tossing to combine. Reduce heat to medium, then cook for 5 to 6 minutes, until the sauce has thickened. Stir in the cashews right before serving. Serve over rice with toppings (if using).

Kitchen Cure: "Crisp-tender" is when a vegetable is cooked but still has a bit of bite or crunch to it.

Italian Stuffed Peppers

Serves 6
Prep time: 15 minutes
Cook time: 50 minutes

3 bell peppers (any color)

1 (15-ounce) can
    chickpeas,
    drained and rinsed

2 cups cooked quinoa

2 cups vegan mozzarella
    cheese shreds, divided

1 (14.5-ounce) can
    fire-roasted diced
    tomatoes

1 tablespoon
    dried oregano

1 teaspoon onion powder

1 teaspoon salt

½ teaspoon garlic powder

¼ teaspoon black pepper

Fresh basil, for topping

Stuffed peppers are fun because they're not only the meal, but also the serving dish! These are definitely small-yet-mighty meals, as they provide a powerful protein punch. I like to serve them with a side of rice and a salad.

1. **Prepare the bell peppers.** Preheat the oven to 375°F. Halve the peppers lengthwise. Remove the seeds and pith, then set, cut-side up, in a 2-quart baking dish.

2. **Mix the filling.** Measure 1 cup of chickpeas (refrigerate the rest for another use). Transfer to a large bowl. Add the quinoa, 1 cup of cheese, the tomatoes and their juices, oregano, onion powder, salt, garlic powder, and black pepper, stirring to combine

3. **Bake.** Scoop the filling into the pepper halves, then top with the remaining 1 cup of cheese. Cover with aluminum foil and bake for 30 minutes. Remove the foil, then bake for another 15 to 20 minutes, until the peppers have softened and the cheese melts. Top with basil before serving.

Did You Know? Quinoa (pronounced *KEEN-wah*) is often referred to as a grain, but it's a seed! It's high in protein and fiber and naturally gluten-free. Rinse your quinoa before cooking it; otherwise, it can have a bitter flavor.

Balsamic-Glazed Veggie and Kale Bowls

Serves 4
Prep time: 15 minutes
Cook time: 30 minutes

For the glazed veggies

3 large carrots

2 red bell peppers

1 head cauliflower

3 tablespoons olive oil

½ teaspoon salt

2 tablespoons balsamic vinegar

2 tablespoons real maple syrup

For the quinoa

1 cup quinoa, rinsed and drained

2 cups water

½ teaspoon garlic powder

½ teaspoon salt

¼ teaspoon black pepper

2 cups packed torn kale leaves

When roasting veggies, use a baking sheet large enough to let them rest in a single layer. If they are stacked, they'll steam rather than roast, and you won't get those lovely golden-brown bits.

1. **Chop the veggies.** Preheat the oven to 350°F. Cut the carrots into ½-inch pieces. Cut the bell peppers into large dice. Cut the cauliflower into florets. Place the veggies on a large baking sheet.

2. **Roast the veggies.** Drizzle the veggies with the oil and sprinkle with salt. Stir to coat, then arrange in a single layer. Bake for 25 to 30 minutes, stirring once halfway through, until tender and golden brown. Turn off the oven. Drizzle the veggies with the vinegar and maple syrup and stir until evenly coated. Return the pan to the oven to keep warm while you assemble the bowls.

3. **Cook the quinoa.** While the veggies roast, in a medium saucepan over high heat, combine the quinoa and water. Bring to a boil, then reduce heat to low. Cover and simmer for 15 minutes, until the water has been absorbed. Remove from the heat, then stir in the garlic powder, salt, and pepper. Stir in the kale and cover. Let sit for 3 to 4 minutes, until the kale wilts.

4. **Assemble the bowls.** Scoop the quinoa mixture into bowls, top with the glazed veggies, and serve.

Mediterranean Chickpea Bowls with Tahini Sauce

Serves 4
Prep time: 20 minutes
Cook time: 1 minute

For the sauce

½ cup tahini
¼ teaspoon salt
¼ teaspoon garlic powder
¼ teaspoon lemon juice

For the salad

2 heads romaine lettuce
2 tomatoes
½ cucumber
¼ cup lemon juice
2 tablespoons olive oil
¼ teaspoon salt
1 (15-ounce) can
    chickpeas,
    rinsed and drained
1 cup Easy Hummus
    (page 42) or
    store-bought
1 (2.25-ounce) can sliced
    black olives, drained
Black pepper

This dish is easy to riff on. Add additional veggies to the salad, like red onion or red bell pepper. Keep in mind the tahini sauce is just meant to be a drizzle on the top, about 2 tablespoons per bowl. If you want more, just double that part of the recipe!

1. **Make the sauce.** In a small bowl, combine the tahini, salt, garlic powder, and lemon juice. Add warm water, 1 tablespoon at a time, while whisking all the ingredients together. You want the sauce to be thin enough to drizzle over the bowl, but not too thin.

2. **Make the salad.** Chop the lettuce into bite-size pieces and measure out 4 cups. Core and dice the tomatoes. Cut the cucumber into large dice. Place all the veggies in a large bowl and toss with the lemon juice, oil, and salt.

3. **Prepare the chickpeas.** In a microwave-safe bowl, heat the chickpeas for 45 to 60 seconds, until warm.

4. **Assemble the bowls.** Build each bowl with equal amounts of the prepared salad. Top each bowl with warm chickpeas, hummus, black olives, and pepper. Drizzle with tahini sauce and serve.

Ingredient Info: Tahini is a paste made from toasted sesame seeds that is widely used in Mediterranean dishes.

Easy Burrito Bowls with Cauliflower Rice

30-MINUTE
GLUTEN-FREE
NUT-FREE
ONE-POT
SOY-FREE

Serves 6
Prep time: 10 minutes
Cook time: 20 minutes

2 (10-ounce) bags frozen
    riced cauliflower

2 tablespoons water

1 tablespoon lime juice

2 teaspoons ground cumin

1 teaspoon salt

1 teaspoon garlic powder

¼ teaspoon black pepper

2 tablespoons olive oil

2 bell peppers (any color),
    cut into 2-inch strips

1 onion, cut into
    2-inch strips

2 (16-ounce) cans
    chili beans

1 cup frozen corn

2 avocados

½ teaspoon salt

Black pepper

Salsa, for topping

These bowls are lighter than a traditional burrito and perfect for when you want a delicious meal that won't weigh you down.

1. **Cook the cauliflower.** In a large nonstick skillet over medium heat, cook the cauliflower in the water, stirring occasionally, for 2 to 3 minutes, until the cauliflower has thawed. Stir in the lime, cumin, salt, garlic powder, and pepper. Cook for about 4 minutes, until heated through. Transfer to a bowl.

2. **Cook the veggies.** In the same skillet over medium-high heat, heat the oil until it shimmers. Add the bell peppers and onion. Cook, stirring occasionally, for 5 to 6 minutes, until tender.

3. **Add the beans.** Pour in the beans with their liquid. Add the corn. Simmer for 2 to 3 minutes or until heated through. Taste and add salt and pepper as needed.

4. **Assemble the bowls.** Scoop an even amount of cauliflower into each bowl, then top with the bean mixture. Carefully halve, pit, and peel the avocados (see page 19). Transfer the fruit to a small bowl and mash with the back of a fork. Stir in the salt, then add a dollop to the top of each burrito bowl, along with salsa. Enjoy!

Thai-Style Peanut Chickpea Salad

30-MINUTE

Serves 4
Prep time: 25 minutes

For the dressing

½ cup creamy
   peanut butter

2 tablespoons lime juice

2 tablespoons soy sauce

1 tablespoon brown sugar

1 to 2 teaspoons sriracha

¼ cup water, as needed

For the salad

3 cups chopped
   romaine lettuce

2 cups thinly sliced
   red cabbage

2 carrots, grated

1 red bell pepper, cut into
   large dice

½ cucumber, sliced and
   quartered

1 (15-ounce) can chick-
   peas, drained and rinsed

This salad is meant to be an entire meal—that's why it's so big! The Thai-style peanut dressing is delicious. It's also great with roasted peanuts. And if you're feeding four extra-hungry people, just double the chickpeas.

1. **Make the dressing.** In a small bowl, whisk together the peanut butter, lime juice, soy sauce, brown sugar, and sriracha. Add water, 1 tablespoon at a time, until you get a pourable consistency. Taste and adjust the seasonings as needed. Set aside.

2. **Make the salad.** In a large serving bowl, combine the lettuce, cabbage, carrots, bell pepper, and cucumber. Add the chickpeas. Pour in about half of the dressing. Toss using salad tongs or two forks until the salad is evenly coated. Add more dressing as desired, or serve with extra on the side. Serve immediately.

Kitchen Cure: You can prepare this salad up to one day in advance. Store the dressing separately from the rest of the ingredients in an airtight container in the fridge, then toss everything together right before serving.

Zesty Peppers and Bowties

This pasta dish will look deceptively simple . . . until you try the sauce! It's zesty and flavorful yet easy to make.

Serves 4
Prep time: 15 minutes
Cook time: 25 minutes

3 tablespoons olive
    oil, divided
2 red bell peppers, sliced
    into ½-inch strips
1 teaspoon minced garlic
8 ounces dried
    farfalle pasta
1 lime
2 tablespoons
    chopped parsley
1 teaspoon
    whole-grain mustard
1 teaspoon real
    maple syrup
½ teaspoon salt
⅛ teaspoon black pepper
1 teaspoon nutritional
    yeast (optional)

1. **Cook the peppers.** In a large saucepan over medium-high heat, heat 2 tablespoons of oil until it shimmers. Add the peppers. Cook for 6 to 7 minutes, until crisp-tender. Add the garlic and cook for 1 to 2 minutes. Transfer to a bowl.

2. **Boil the pasta.** Fill the pan with salted water and return to high heat. Add the pasta and cook according to package instructions until tender, usually about 10 minutes. Reserve 1 cup of cooking liquid, then drain.

3. **Make the sauce.** While the pasta cooks, use the palm of your hand to roll the lime over a cutting board to loosen the juices. Zest the lime into a small bowl, then halve it and squeeze the juice into the bowl. Add the parsley, mustard, maple syrup, salt, pepper, remaining 1 tablespoon of oil, and 1 to 2 tablespoons of cooking liquid. Whisk to combine.

4. **Combine.** Return the drained pasta to the hot pan. Add the pepper mixture and sauce. Place over low heat for 2 to 3 minutes, until warmed through. If you want it a little saucier, stir in another 1 to 2 tablespoons of cooking liquid. Taste and add more salt and pepper as needed. Serve topped with nutritional yeast (if using).

Banh Mi-Inspired Veggie Dogs

Serves 4
Prep time: 10 minutes, plus 1 hour to pickle
Cook time: 5 minutes

1 medium carrot
1 small jicama (smaller than an apple)
1 jalapeño pepper
½ cup rice wine vinegar
3 tablespoons sugar
½ teaspoon sesame oil
½ teaspoon salt
4 veggie dogs
4 hot dog buns, warmed
Sriracha, for serving (optional)

Banh mi sandwiches are a Vietnamese staple, usually made with meat topped with pickled veggies, cilantro, and super spicy sauce. While this version isn't authentic, it's definitely a delicious, fun take on veggie dogs.

1. **Prepare the vegetables.** Grate the carrot. Dice the jicama. Remove the seeds and pith from the jalapeño, then dice what remains.

2. **Pickle the vegetables.** In a shallow bowl, whisk together the vinegar, sugar, sesame oil, and salt. Add the carrot and jicama, cover, and refrigerate for at least 1 hour, stirring once or twice.

3. **Top and serve.** When you're ready to serve, heat the veggie dogs per package instructions, usually pricked with a fork and then microwaved for about 2 minutes. Place the dogs in the buns and top with the pickled veggies. Sprinkle the jalapeño over the tops, then drizzle with sriracha (if using). Enjoy!

Change It Up: Serve with a side of French fries, and mix 1 to 2 teaspoons of sriracha with ½ cup ketchup for dipping.

Chocolate Mug Cakes, page 118

CHAPTER 6

Desserts and Drinks

Cinnamon Twists with Cream Cheese Dip

30-MINUTE

Serves 4
Prep time: 15 minutes
Cook time: 10 minutes

For the twists

Nonstick spray

1 tube Pillsbury crescent
roll dough

3 tablespoons
vegan butter

¼ teaspoon vanilla extract

2 tablespoons plus
1 teaspoon granu-
lated sugar

1½ teaspoons ground
cinnamon

For the dip

6 ounces vegan
cream cheese, room
temperature

1 cup powdered sugar

½ teaspoon vanilla extract

1 to 2 tablespoons
unsweetened
nondairy milk

Inspired by churros, these cinnamon twists will make your kitchen smell amazing!

1. **Prepare the dough.** Preheat the oven to 375°F. Lightly coat a baking sheet with nonstick spray. Unroll the dough onto the baking sheet, separate into four rectangles, and pinch together the triangle seams.

2. **Melt the butter.** In a microwave-safe dish, micro-wave the butter in 5-second bursts until melted. Stir in the vanilla. In a separate small bowl, stir together the granulated sugar and cinnamon.

3. **Flavor the dough.** Spread half the vanilla-butter mixture evenly across two of the dough rectangles with a spoon, then sprinkle with half of the sugar mixture. Cover with the two remaining (unbuttered) rectangles. Pinch the edges together around all four sides of both rectangles.

4. **Cut and twist.** Slice the rectangles, crosswise, into six strips each. Place next to each other after slicing, and spoon the remaining butter and sugar mix-ture over them. Holding each end, twist each strip, then place on the baking sheet with at least ½ inch between each.

5. **Bake.** Bake for 6 to 8 minutes, until a light golden brown.

6. **Make the dip.** While the twists bake, stir together the cream cheese, powdered sugar, and vanilla. Add 1 tablespoon of milk at a time to get a dippable con-sistency. Serve with the warm twists.

Chocolate and Peanut Butter Pretzel Bark

Serves 4

Prep time: 10 minutes, plus 30 minutes to chill

Cook time: 5 minutes

½ cup pretzels

1 cup water

½ cup vegan chocolate chips

½ teaspoon coconut oil

3 tablespoons creamy peanut butter

Pretzel bark is easy to make and delicious on its own, but I like to serve mine crumbled over a big bowl of vanilla ice cream!

1. **Break the pretzels.** Line a baking sheet with parchment paper and set aside. Place the pretzels in a zip-top bag and seal it. Place flat on the counter, then use a pot to whack the bag a few times until the pretzels are unevenly broken. Set aside.

2. **Melt the chocolate.** In a small saucepan over high heat, bring the water to a boil. Place a small heat-proof bowl over the water (but not touching it). This is called a double boiler and is the safest way to melt chocolate. Turn off the heat and add the chocolate chips and oil to the bowl. Let sit, uncovered, for 1 to 2 minutes, then stir gently with a rubber spatula. If the water gets cold and the chocolate stops melting, turn the heat back on low for a minute. Continue until the chocolate is fully melted.

3. **Pour.** Pour the chocolate sauce into an even ¼-inch-thick layer on the prepared baking sheet. Let cool while preparing the peanut butter.

4. **Melt the peanut butter.** Place the peanut butter in a microwave-safe dish and microwave for 30 to 60 seconds, until liquid. Use a spoon to swirl it all over the chocolate. Sprinkle the pretzels evenly over the top.

5. **Chill.** Place the entire baking sheet in the refrigerator for at least 30 minutes, until it's set. Break into smaller pieces and enjoy.

Apples 'n' Caramel Dip

30-MINUTE
GLUTEN-FREE
ONE-POT
SOY-FREE

Serves 4
Prep time: 10 minutes
Cook time: 10 minutes

¾ cup coconut cream

¾ cup packed light
   brown sugar

4 tablespoons light
   corn syrup

1 tablespoon cornstarch

3 tablespoons
   vegan butter

1 teaspoon vanilla extract

4 large Granny
   Smith apples

I went to the carnival each summer as a child, and I always begged for a caramel apple. Each time I thought it was going to be the most magical treat, and each time I was disappointed because it was difficult to eat! Now that I'm older and wiser, I keep the caramel in a bowl and dip the apple slices in, and it's so much better this way.

1. **Make the dip.** In a medium saucepan over low heat, combine the coconut cream, brown sugar, corn syrup, and cornstarch. Whisk constantly for 6 to 7 minutes, until the coconut cream melts. Remove from the heat and stir in the butter and vanilla, until the butter melts. Set aside while you prepare the apples.

2. **Slice the apples.** Cut the apples into wedges, removing the core. Serve the dip in individual ramekins with apples on the side.

Ingredient Info: Before measuring the coconut cream, be sure to stir together the liquids and solids completely.

Strawberry Cheesecake Ice Cream Pie

Serves 4 to 6

Prep time: 15 minutes, plus 2 hours to freeze

1 pint vegan strawberry ice cream

8 ounces plain vegan cream cheese

2 tablespoons sugar

1 (6-ounce) premade graham cracker crust

1½ cups sliced straw-berries (optional)

I love cheesecake, but I don't always want to spend that much time making a dessert. This "pie" was inspired by that yummy, sweet cream cheese flavor and my all-time favorite ice cream: straw-berry. You can use any flavor of ice cream you love, and I bet it would still be delicious!

1. **Make the filling.** Remove the cover from the ice cream and let it sit on the counter for 15 minutes to soften. Meanwhile, in a medium bowl, stir the cream cheese and sugar until combined. A wooden spoon works great for this step. When the ice cream is softened, add it to the bowl and stir, but not too much! You don't want it combined completely; instead you want thick swirls.

2. **Fill the piecrust.** Spoon the ice cream mixture into the piecrust, using the back of the spoon to press it down gently. (Don't worry if you break the crust—it will still be delicious!) When it's spread evenly and the top is pretty smooth, cover the pie and place it in the freezer for at least 2 hours to chill. Serve topped with the strawberries (if using).

Kitchen Cure: Move the pie into the fridge about 15 minutes before you're ready to serve—it's easier to cut into slices when the ice cream has softened a little.

Cookies 'n' Cream Ice Cream Cake

5 INGREDIENT
30-MINUTE
ONE-POT

Serves 4

Prep time: 20 minutes, plus 3 hours to freeze

20 vegan sandwich cookies, such as Oreos, divided

2 tablespoons vegan butter, melted

3 cups vegan vanilla ice cream, softened

½ cup vegan chocolate syrup, such as Hershey's Simply 5

1 to 2 cups coconut whipped topping

When I was growing up, ice cream cakes were a dessert I asked for often—there is just something about that vanilla and chocolate combination. This version is easy to make, and I hope you'll enjoy it as much as I do.

1. **Prepare the pan.** Line a 9-by-5-inch loaf pan with aluminum foil, with 2 to 3 inches of overhang along the long sides of the pan. This will help you lift the cake out when it's time to slice.

2. **Make the cookie layer.** Place 15 cookies in a food processor and pulse until crumbled. Stir in the melted butter until combined, then transfer to the prepared pan. Press the cookies firmly and evenly into the bottom of the pan.

3. **Add the ice cream and freeze.** Spoon in the ice cream and spread evenly over the cookie crust. Drizzle with the chocolate syrup. Cover and freeze for 2 hours.

4. **Add the topping.** Quarter the remaining cookies. Uncover the cake and top with the whipped topping and cookie pieces. Cover and freeze for at least 1 hour. Remove from the freezer 15 minutes before serving.

Kitchen Cure: No food processor? No problem! Break the cookies in half and place into a large zip-top bag. Seal tight and lay flat on the countertop. Hit repeatedly with a rolling pin until the cookies are in small crumbles.

Gingersnap Apple Pie Sundaes

30-MINUTE
NUT-FREE
ONE-POT
SOY-FREE

Serves 4
Prep time: 15 minutes
Cook time: 15 minutes

For the pie filling

4 Honeycrisp apples

2 tablespoons
vegan butter

2 tablespoons
brown sugar

1 teaspoon ground
cinnamon

½ teaspoon lemon juice

¼ teaspoon ground ginger

For the sundaes

8 to 10 vegan ginger-
snap cookies

8 scoops vegan vanilla
ice cream

Coconut whipped topping
(optional)

Many brands of gingersnap cookies are "acci-dentally vegan" and make a delicious crust. This dessert makes the perfect ending to a special meal, without all the work that goes into a tradi-tional apple pie! Since it's so easy to make, it would also be great for a DIY sundae party with your friends.

1. **Make the pie filling.** Peel the apples and cut into bite-size pieces. In a saucepan over medium heat, melt the butter, then add the apples, sugar, cinnamon, lemon juice, and ginger. Stir until combined. Cover and reduce the heat to low. Cook, stirring occasion-ally, for 12 to 15 minutes, until the apples are soft. Remove from the heat and cool for 2 to 3 minutes.

2. **Crumble the cookies.** Meanwhile, use your hands to break the cookies into smaller pieces (thirds or fourths).

3. **Assemble the sundaes.** Add the ice cream to the bowls first, followed by the apple mixture and then the cookie pieces. Top with whipped topping (if using). Enjoy!

Kitchen Cure: The apple mixture can be made up to a day in advance and kept refrigerated in an airtight container. Simply microwave it for 45 to 60 seconds to warm it up before serving.

Chocolate Mug Cakes

Serves 4
Prep time: 10 minutes
Cook time: 4 minutes

For the frosting

1¼ cups powdered sugar

⅓ cup vegan butter

½ teaspoon vanilla extract

⅛ teaspoon salt

For the cakes

½ cup cocoa powder

½ cup all-purpose flour

½ cup granulated sugar

½ teaspoon
   baking powder

½ teaspoon salt

¼ cup unsweetened
   applesauce

¾ cup unsweetened
   nondairy milk

1 tablespoon
   vanilla extract

Chocolate cake in less than 15 minutes? Yes, please! These individual cakes are perfectly sized for a quick treat. They are easy to make, and since you eat them directly out of the mug, there are even fewer dishes to clean afterward.

1. **Make the frosting.** In a medium bowl, combine the powdered sugar, butter, vanilla, and salt. Use a hand mixer to beat the ingredients together, starting at low speed and then increasing to medium-high. Beat until just smooth. Set aside.

2. **Mix the dry ingredients.** In a separate medium bowl, stir together the cocoa powder, flour, granulated sugar, baking powder, and salt until combined.

3. **Mix the wet ingredients.** In a small bowl, stir together the applesauce, milk, and vanilla, then add to the dry ingredients. Stir until completely combined.

4. **Microwave the cakes.** Pour the batter evenly into four 10- to 15-ounce mugs. Microwave each mug (one at a time!) for 60 to 70 seconds. Top each with a dollop of frosting and enjoy!

Change It Up: Don't have time to make frosting? Some brands of premade frosting you can buy at the store are accidentally vegan, or you could top with coconut whipped topping!

The Best Strawberry Milkshakes

5 INGREDIENT
30-MINUTE
GLUTEN-FREE
ONE-POT
SOY-FREE

Serves 4
Prep time: 10 minutes

1 (12-ounce) package
fresh strawberries

1 cup unsweetened
cashew milk, divided

1 pint vegan vanilla
ice cream

Strawberry milkshakes have always been, and will always be, my number one favorite dessert. I'll never tire of them, but if you do, check out the tip at the end for some other flavor ideas!

1. **Chill the glasses.** Place four glasses in the freezer to chill.

2. **Prepare the strawberries.** Hull the strawberries, then cut them into quarters. Add them all to a blender, along with ½ cup of milk. Pulse until there are no large pieces left.

3. **Blend.** Add the ice cream and blend until just smooth. You don't want the ice cream to melt too much. Add the milk, 2 to 3 tablespoons at a time, as needed to get the consistency you like. Serve in the chilled glasses.

Change It Up: Strawberries not in season? Try blueberries, cherries, or even peaches!

Sweet Basil Lemonade

5 INGREDIENT
30-MINUTE
GLUTEN-FREE
NUT-FREE
ONE-POT
SOY-FREE

Serves 4

Prep time: 10 minutes, plus overnight to steep

4 lemons

4 cups water

¼ cup plus 2 tablespoons real maple syrup

10 fresh basil leaves, torn in half

Ice, for serving

Here's a completely different take on lemonade, one with a bit more complexity. I recommend pairing it with a dish that's also made with basil.

1. **Juice the lemons.** Roll the lemons across a flat surface using your palm to loosen the juice, then halve them. If you have a citrus juicer, use that to juice the lemons. If not, stick the tines of a fork into the lemon half while you squeeze, slowly twisting the fork. Do this over a fine-mesh strainer to catch the seeds. Measure out ½ cup.

2. **Combine.** In a pitcher, stir together the water, lemon juice, maple syrup, and basil leaves. Cover and refrigerate to steep overnight.

3. **Remove the basil leaves.** Pour the lemonade through a fine-mesh strainer into a pitcher to remove the basil leaves, then serve over ice. Enjoy!

Hot Cocoa

5 INGREDIENT
30-MINUTE
GLUTEN-FREE
ONE-POT
SOY-FREE

Mm-mm, hot chocolate. It's part drink, part dessert, and 100 percent comforting! Whether you're enjoying this after a snowball fight or while relaxing in the evening, it's even better if you add a dollop of coconut whipped topping.

Serves 4

Prep time: 10 minutes

Cook time: 10 minutes

4 cups unsweetened cashew milk

¼ cup sugar

3 tablespoons unsweet- ened cocoa powder

½ cup vegan chocolate chips

¼ teaspoon vanilla extract

Coconut whipped topping (optional)

1. **Heat the milk.** In a medium saucepan over medium-high heat, combine the milk, sugar, and cocoa powder. Whisk for 3 to 4 minutes, until you can feel heat coming from the liquid, but don't allow it to boil.

2. **Melt the chocolate chips.** Reduce the heat to low. Add the chocolate chips. Continue to stir until the chips melt, about 5 minutes, then add the vanilla. Pour into mugs and top with coconut whipped topping (if using). Enjoy!

Pineapple-Strawberry Slushies

This refreshing drink will make you feel like you're lying on a beach, even if you make it in the middle of winter. I think it's so pretty with the two layers of color and flavor. By blending the (lighter) pineapple first, there's no need to rinse the blender out in between steps 2 and 3!

Serves 4
Prep time: 10 minutes

3 cups fresh strawberries

3 cups frozen pineapple chunks

2 teaspoons real maple syrup, divided

1 teaspoon lemon juice, divided

2 cups ice, divided

1. **Hull the strawberries.** Remove the tops of the strawberries, then halve them.

2. **Blend the pineapple.** In the blender, combine the pineapple, 1 teaspoon of maple syrup, and ½ teaspoon of lemon juice. Pulse twice, then add ½ cup of ice and pulse 2 to 3 more times. You want the ice in small pieces but not liquefied. Pour the pineapple mixture into four glasses.

3. **Blend the strawberries.** Add the strawberries to the blender with the remaining 1 teaspoon of maple syrup and ½ teaspoon of lemon juice. Pulse until it forms a puree. Add the remaining 1½ cups of ice and pulse 1 to 2 times more until the ice is in small pieces, same as with the pineapple.

4. **Serve.** Pour the strawberry mixture over the pineapple mixture in the glasses and serve with reusable straws.

Change It Up: Try replacing the pineapple with frozen blueberries, or the strawberries with raspberries!

Raspberry Iced Tea

Serves 4
Prep time: 10 minutes
Cook time: 5 minutes

8 cups water

⅔ cup sugar

3 black tea bags

1 (12-ounce) bag frozen
raspberries, thawed

1 tablespoon lemon juice

Using frozen raspberries allows you to make this refreshing drink year-round. When they are in season, though, fresh ones can't be beat!

1. **Boil.** In a large saucepan, combine the water and sugar over high heat. Bring to a boil and stir for about 1 minute, until the sugar is dissolved. Remove from the heat.

2. **Steep.** If the tea bags have tags, remove them. Add the tea bags and raspberries to the hot sugar water. Cover and let sit for 3 to 4 minutes.

3. **Strain.** Pour the tea from the pan through a fine-mesh strainer into a pitcher. Stir in the lemon juice and chill until ready to serve.

Blueberry Lemonade

5 INGREDIENT
30-MINUTE
GLUTEN-FREE
NUT-FREE
ONE-POT
SOY-FREE

Serves 4

Prep time: 15 minutes

4 lemons

2 cups fresh blue-
berries, divided

⅓ cup sugar

4 cups water, divided

Ice, for serving

I remember my grandmother making lemonade for me when I was a little girl. It was the kind made from a powdered mix, but I didn't care. That lemon flavor tasted like summer to me, and I always asked for more. This homemade blueberry version is just as good as I remember, and I always add that extra bit of lemon juice at the end because I like mine tart!

1. **Juice the lemons.** Roll the lemons across a flat surface using your palm to loosen the juice, then halve them. If you have a citrus juicer, use that to juice the lemons. If not, stick the tines of a fork into the lemon half while you squeeze, slowly twisting the fork. Do this over a fine-mesh strainer to catch the seeds. Measure out ½ cup, plus 2 tablespoons.

2. **Blend.** Combine 1½ cups of blueberries, the sugar, ½ cup of lemon juice, and 2 cups of water in a blender. Blend until it is a smooth puree. Pour the mixture through a fine-mesh strainer into a pitcher to remove any solids.

3. **Make the lemonade.** Stir in another 1½ to 2 cups of water and the remaining ½ cup of blueberries. Taste and stir in the remaining 2 tablespoons of lemon juice, one at a time, if you want a tarter drink. Refrigerate until cold, then serve over ice.

Change It Up: If you like bubbles, or just want to make your batch of lemonade serve more people, try stirring in your favorite lemon-lime soda or seltzer water.

Maraschino Cherry Sparklers

Serves 4
Prep time: 5 minutes

3 cups lemon-lime
   flavored soda or
   seltzer water

1 cup orange juice

3 tablespoons grena-
   dine syrup

2 tablespoons cherry
   syrup (or more)

Ice, for serving

Maraschino cherries,
   for topping

This sparkling, fruity drink will make even the warmest summer days seem just a bit cooler.

1. **Mix the drink.** In a pitcher, use a long-handled spoon to stir together the soda, orange juice, grenadine, and cherry syrup. Taste, then add an additional tablespoon of cherry syrup if you want more cherry flavor.

2. **Serve and enjoy.** Fill four glasses about three-fourths full with ice cubes. Pour the drink over the ice and top with cherries. Serve immediately.

Ingredient Info: Grenadine syrup is made from pomegranates and has a bright, tart flavor. Combined with the cherry syrup, it keeps the drink from being too sweet.

Avocado Smoothies

5 INGREDIENT
30-MINUTE
GLUTEN-FREE
ONE-POT

Serves 4
Prep time: 5 minutes

1 large avocado
2 ripe bananas
3½ cups unsweetened
    nondairy milk
1 cup baby spinach
1 cup ice
½ teaspoon vanilla extract

I love smoothies; they make a great treat. If you're serving this as a meal replacement, consider adding 1 to 2 scoops of your favorite vegan protein powder. And if you'd like it a little sweeter, try adding 1 to 2 tablespoons of real maple syrup.

1. **Combine.** Carefully halve, pit, and peel the avocado (see page 19). Peel the bananas. Add the avocado and bananas to a blender along with the milk, spinach, ice, and vanilla.

2. **Blend.** Blend on high until smooth. You may need to use a rubber spatula to scrape down the sides of the blender. If you want to make it thinner, add another 1 to 2 tablespoons of milk. Enjoy!

Ingredient Info: If you make a lot of smoothies, keep peeled, sliced bananas in your freezer. They can take the place of ice and keep your smoothies from getting watered down. Store them in an airtight container, and they'll last for up to two weeks.

Berry Yummy Smoothies

30-MINUTE
GLUTEN-FREE
ONE-POT

Serves 4
Prep time: 5 minutes

2 ripe bananas

2 cups sweetened or
unsweetened nondairy
milk (or more)

1 cup frozen strawberries

1 cup frozen blueberries

1 cup frozen raspberries

1½ cups plain or vanilla
vegan yogurt

Frozen fruit is always best for smoothies. It makes the drink cold without using ice, which can water it down. To make it easier, you can also just use 3 cups of frozen mixed berries. See the tip for the Avocado Smoothies recipe (page 127) to learn about freezing bananas, too!

1. **Combine.** Peel and halve the bananas. Transfer to a blender along with the milk, strawberries, blueberries, raspberries, and yogurt.

2. **Blend.** Blend until smooth. If the smoothie is too thick, add more milk, 1 tablespoon at a time. Enjoy!

Measurement Conversions

VOLUME EQUIVALENTS	U.S. STANDARD	U.S. STANDARD (OUNCES)	METRIC (APPROXIMATE)
LIQUID	2 tablespoons	1 fl. oz.	30 mL
	¼ cup	2 fl. oz.	60 mL
	½ cup	4 fl. oz.	120 mL
	1 cup	8 fl. oz.	240 mL
	1½ cups	12 fl. oz.	355 mL
	2 cups or 1 pint	16 fl. oz.	475 mL
	4 cups or 1 quart	32 fl. oz.	1 L
	1 gallon	128 fl. oz.	4 L
DRY	⅛ teaspoon		0.5 mL
	¼ teaspoon		1 mL
	½ teaspoon		2 mL
	¾ teaspoon		4 mL
	1 teaspoon		5 mL
	1 tablespoon		15 mL
	¼ cup		59 mL
	⅛ cup		79 mL
	½ cup		118 mL
	2/8 cup		156 mL
	¾ cup		177 mL
	1 cup		235 mL
	2 cups or 1 pint		475 mL
	3 cups		700 mL
	4 cups or 1 quart		1 L
	½ gallon		2 L
	1 gallon		4 L

OVEN TEMPERATURES

FAHRENHEIT	CELSIUS (APPROXIMATE)
250°F	120°C
300°F	150°C
325°F	165°C
350°F	180°C
375°F	190°C
400°F	200°C
425°F	220°C
450°F	230°C

WEIGHT EQUIVALENTS

U.S. STANDARD	METRIC (APPROXIMATE)
½ ounce	15 g
1 ounce	30 g
2 ounces	60 g
4 ounces	115 g
8 ounces	225 g
12 ounces	340 g
16 ounces or 1 pound	455 g

Index

Acknowledgments

Writing a cookbook takes a lot of time and effort, but I am so grateful for the opportunity to share my love of vegan food and all the ways home cooks can make the world better for animals. The animals are why I am vegan, and why I try to encourage everyone to eat more plant-based meals.

That said, I didn't write this cookbook alone! My mom, my number one supporter and cheerleader, was always there to help chop veggies and wash the never-ending stream of dirty dishes. Denise Lindom, friend/sous-chef/drinking partner, is the best for bouncing flavor and ingredient ideas off of—and has been since my very first book! Sharon Meyer and Sherri Maxwell provided the emotional support and girls' ski trips that kept me sane. I'm lucky to be surrounded by such wonderful women!

My recipe testing team deserves so many thanks, as always. Erin "Baking Guru" Burgmaier, Susan Burgmaier, Brooke Dunn, Sherri Maxwell, Cynthia Thayer, and Velma Wagner—THANK YOU!

I can't leave out my best furry family members: Elmer (RIP), Chico, and Charlie. The snuggles and kisses you give fill my heart.

Last but definitely not least, thank you to Andrea Leptinsky, Jessica Easto, and the entire Callisto team. You make me feel like the best cookbook author in the world!

About the Author

Barb Musick lives in Colorado with her pack of rescue pets. She shares her adventures and love of food, travel, and animals on her blog, *That Was Vegan?*, along with vegan recipes everyone will love. This is her fifth cookbook. Visit her at ThatWasVegan.com.

CPSIA information can be obtained
at www.ICGtesting.com
Printed in the USA
LVHW070815260721
693626LV00024B/1812

9 781648 760280